IN THE BEGINNING THE HEAVENS AND EARTH AS CREATED

PETER LENGWE

All Scripture quotations are taken from the New King James Version® (NKJV).

Printed in the United States of America

ISBN:
Softcover: 978-1-972299-30-2
Hardback: 978-1-972299-31-9
eBook: 978-1-972299-29-6

For permission requests, visit and write to the publisher at:

Peter Lengwe | THE BREAD OF LIFE GLOBAL MINISTRIES

Table of Contents

Acknowledgments

I would like to thank, first and foremost, God my Father, my Lord and Savior, Jesus Christ, for His mercy and grace upon me. I can do nothing without my Lord, who strengthens me and gave me the grace and wisdom to write this book. I have come to the understanding that I am nothing without my God, my Lord and Savior, Jesus Christ, because I do not seek my own glory and will but the glory and will of God Almighty, my Father, whom I stand before in awe, giving Him thanks and all the praise, all the glory, and all the honor with all that I am—spirit, soul, and body. I love you, Father, and may Your will be done in the name of Jesus Christ, my Lord, so that this book gets to those whom You intend to reach, and I pray that You open their minds to understanding so that they can comprehend what is spiritual because Your word is spiritually discerned.

I am appreciative and grateful for my new church home and pastor for the support and encouragement given to me in my spiritual walk.

I would also like to thank Susan D'Amato for answering the call of God to help me with the editing and typing of this book. May the good Lord, God, bless you in health and prosper you in all the desires of your heart. I am forever thankful.

And to my publisher, Xulon, much appreciation and gratitude for all the guidance, suggestions, and overall review you gave me, for which I was humbly brought to tears.

And to those who will read this book, I thank you in advance, and I pray that it may enrich you spiritually and grow you in the ways of God, to help you love God and live by faith in His righteousness in Christ Jesus. For those who don't know Jesus Christ, I pray that you may find Him and know Him so that you may receive salvation into the kingdom of God. The word of God is Life everlasting.

INTRODUCTION

After coming to Christ and being born again, I got what I had asked for, which is for the Lord, God, to teach me His word. I started studying the word of God and the spirit gave me understanding of His word, and I became captivated and I fell in love with it. To be clear, I am not claiming to know it all but what the spirit has allowed me to know, and I am still craving to know more, for we are all given a measure of faith and grace according to the desire of the spirit of God. The burden was what to do with all the revelation I had received from the Holy Spirit. I had only two ways to go about it: the first one was to preach it and the second one was to write about it. The first one seems obvious to me, but the Lord has not opened that door yet, so I was left with the second one.

I never thought I would ever write a book in my life. One thing you have to know is that I have never attended college; this is only by the grace of God and not at all my doing. I am just a vessel being directed and guided by the Spirit of God. Then I had two ways to go about it, whether to write about the beginning of the creation of the world age or the end of this world age. The obvious was to write about the beginning of creation, hence this book. The foundation of my book is 2 Peter 3:5–7, and my purpose was to outline in a profound way comparing and proving scripture with scripture in the simplest way—that there are three world ages, according to the word of God. I explain in depth, in a way that is both thoughtful and thought-provoking, and by provoking our hearts and minds, my hope and prayer is that we may seek the truth from God by bringing discussion of many to the table regarding the truth of what was, what is now, and what is yet to come.

God, we need the truth to be told more so in this generation where the truth is being subverted or replaced with false doctrine and false worship. That is why I go in depth to explain what God's plan was then and what God's plan is now and what God's plan is for the future. Within the context, I share briefly my own life experiences, hoping to inspire those who are seeking the truth; the truth of life is only found in God through His word who is Jesus Christ, the Lord. Revelation 19:13 says, ***And He (the Lord, Jesus Christ) was clothed with a vesture dipped in blood: and his name is called The Word of God.*** It is my prayer and hope that this book will turn your hearts and minds to God for the truth and not to this world. God bless you all, first and foremost, that your hearts and minds be renewed and turned only to the heavenly things that are everlasting and not of this world age that are about to be destroyed.

Assistant's Note

How happy I am to have helped Peter in editing and typing his book!

I think it's very fun to mention a little testimony here, what I call a little "God wink." My husband and I have been attending Victory World Outreach Church for three years, and it had been put on my mind, and heart, to offer any kind of typing and/or editing of notes, letters, bulletins, etc. So I finally reached out to our pastor, Blake Andrews, about my offer. That very afternoon on the same day was when the author of this book, Peter, asked Pastor Blake if he knew of someone who could help him edit and type up his book! God wink, and confirmation that this was meant to be.

It really has been my privilege and honor to assist Peter in this endeavor. God bless him and everyone who reads this book!

~ Susan D'Amato ~

CHAPTER 1:
A LITTLE BACKGROUND

For us to really understand what the Apostle Peter, fully inspired by the Spirit of God, was writing to the Christian Jews of the diaspora then, but more so now, to all believers in Christ of who is the head of the church of God which is by His grace given onto us through His Son, our Lord Jesus Christ, we need to equally divide the word of truth comparing scripture with scripture.

2 Timothy 2:15 (LEB)—***Make every effort to present yourself approved to God, a worker having no need to be ashamed, guiding the word of truth along a straight path.*** It's by the grace of God only that I'm able to write this book, because I'm not ashamed of the word of truth, I'm not ashamed to call God my Father, and I'm not ashamed to call Jesus Christ my only Lord and Savior, and I'm surely not ashamed of the Good News (the Gospels) about Jesus Christ. My faith and love in Christ Jesus have given me an appetite for his word. I love his word and live by his word by faith, which all believers in Christ Jesus should.

Now let's look at 2 Peter 3:5–7, which is the foundation on which I base this book.

2 Peter 3:5—*For when they maintain this, it escapes their notice that the heavens existed long ago and the earth held together out of water and through water by the word of God.*
2 Peter 3:6—*That by means of these things, the world that existed at that time was destroyed by being inundated with water.*
2 Peter 3:7—*But by the same word, the present heavens and earth are reserved for fire, being kept for the day of judgement and destruction of ungodly people.*

The background to these three verses is that the Apostle Peter was reminding the Christian Jews of what was to come in the last days: there will be mockers (false teachers) who will come walking in their mockery to distort the promise and the prophecy concerning the coming Messiah and, by so doing, causing many to apostasy (fall away) from the faith.

The term "last days" is very broad. That is, it may mean the time or dispensation from prophesy of the seed of the woman made by God himself.

Genesis 3:15—*And I will put enmity between thee (Satan) and the woman (Eve) and between thy seed (Satan's seed, Cain) and her seed (Jesus Christ). He (Jesus Christ) shall bruise thy head (Satan's head) and thou shalt bruise His heel (Jesus Christ's) heel.*

This dispensation of time extends to the fathers, who are Abraham, Isaac, Jacob, and the twelve sons of Jacob, and all the way through the prophets, and who also embrace the first and second coming of the messiah. This is what the Apostle Peter was implying in referring to the Old Testament, but in the New Testament it is used to define the period of time from the death and resurrection of Jesus Christ to His second coming to judge the ungodly.

Now since we have the background to 2 Peter 3:5–7, let's look at verses 5–7 in detail. These mockers (false teachers) maintain in their minds that things continued the same just as they had been from the beginning of creation, and even after the fathers fell asleep then until now. This thing has been hidden from their will to determine that the heavens existed long ago, the earth (land) left standing and held together out of water and through water by the word of God. Therefore, the Logos of God denoting a word or saying as the expression of thought wherefore not rhema, which denotes a word or saying, or sentence in its outward form as made up of words. Whereby the world (cosmos) consisting of the universe and the earth that then existed at that time, the world as created and arranged. This is the heavens and the earth of Genesis 1:1—*In the beginning God (Elohim plural: the Father, the Son and the Spirit) created (that which preexisted from nothing), the heavens (the sky and all that is in it) and the earth (consisting together of water and through water).* This is the beginning of all physical matter; therefore the first and absolute commencement of the physical universe and this is to the world that then was—2 Peter 3:6.

This beginning should be contrasted with the beginning of John 1:1 KJV, which is: *In the beginning was the Word, and the Word was with God, and the Word was God.*

This beginning in John 1:1 was preexistent before the beginning of Genesis 1:1. The word (Logos) who is Jesus Christ has always been before the ages began, because the ages and the heavens and the earth were prepared by him. Hebrews 1:2 KJV—*Hath in these last days spoken unto us by His Son whom he hath appointed heir of all things, by whom also he made the worlds (ages).* And Hebrews 11:3 KJV says—*Through faith we understand that the worlds (ages) were framed (prepared) by the word (rhema) of God so that things which are seen were not made of things which do appear (visible).* Everything that was and is, and is to come was prepared by the Lord God before the world that then was Genesis 1:1. One thing we have to understand is that before anything became manifest in the physical, they preexisted or existed first in the spirit, therefore the unseen. And this is why it's important to know also that we existed before in a spiritual form before God made our earthly bodies. We are a spirit soul and body (earthly). 1 Thessalonians 5:23 says, *And the very God of peace sanctify you wholly; and I pray God your whole spirit and soul and body be preserved blameless unto the coming of our Lord Jesus Christ.*

CHAPTER 2:
THE WAY IT WAS

Now that we have established the background to 2 Peter 3:5-7, let us look at the heavens and the earth that then was, which is the heavens and earth as created by God in Genesis 1:1, comparing scripture with scripture.

2 Peter 3:5 KJV says—***For this they deliberately forget and are willingly ignorant of that by the word of God (Logos) that the heavens were of old (existed) and the earth standing (held together) out of water and through water.*** This describes the heavens and the earth of Genesis 1:1. To support this scripture, let us look at other scriptures.

Psalms 24:2 says—***For He hath founded it (the world as inhabited) upon the seas and established (to stand) it upon the floods (waters).*** And Psalms 136:6 says—***To him that stretched out the earth (land) above the waters.*** Psalm 104:5 says—***who laid the foundation of the earth (land) that it should not be removed (moved) forever (and ever).*** The word "foundation" has two connotations in the Bible, the first one being:

Before the foundation of the world (cosmos) it occurs three times in the Bible: John 17:24, Ephesians 1:4, and 1 Peter 1:20. The number three means divine perfection or completeness.

The term, "before the foundation of the world" refers to the mystery or secret of God and is connected to the purpose of God. John 17:24 KJV tells us—*Father, I will that they also, whom thou hast given me, be with me where I am; that they may behold my glory, which thou hast given me; for thou lovedst me before the foundation of the world.* Ephesians 1:4 states—*According as he hath chosen us in him before the foundation of the world, that we should be holy and without blame before him in love.* And finally, 1 Peter 1:20 says—*Who verily was foreordained before the foundation of the world, but was manifest in these last times for you.*

The second one comes from the foundation of the world (cosmos); it occurs seven times in the Bible:

1. Luke 11:50—*Therefore this generation will be held responsible for the blood of all the prophets that has been shed since the beginning of the world.*

2. Hebrews 9:26—*Otherwise Christ would have had to suffer many times since the creation of the world. But he has appeared once for all at the culmination of the ages.*

3. Revelations 13:8—*And all the people who belong to this world worshiped the beast.*

4. Matthew 25:34—*Then the King will say to those on his right, Come, you who are blessed by my Father; take your inheritance, the kingdom prepared for you since the creation of the world.*

5. Hebrews 4:3—*Now we who have believed enter that rest, just as God has said, "So I declared on oath in my anger, 'They shall never enter my rest.'" And yet his.*

6. Matthew 13:35—*So was fulfilled what was spoken through the prophet: "I will open my mouth in parables; I will utter things hidden since the creation of the world."*

7. Revelation 17:8—*The beast, which you saw, once was, now is not, and yet will come up out of the Abyss and go to its destruction. The inhabitants of the earth whose names have not been written in the book of life from the creation of the world will be astonished when they see the beast, because he once was, now is not, and yet will come.*

The number seven means spiritual perfection or completeness, and the phrase "from the foundation of the world" refers to His Kingdom and is connected to the counsels or plans of God.

Now everything that God created and made, he foreknew and preordained and predestined before the foundation of the world, just as he foreknew us and chose us before the foundation of the world. Ephesians 1:4 KJV—*According as he hath chosen us in him before the foundation of the world, that we should be holy and without blame before him in love.* This is the foreknowledge of God, therefore the forethought of the all-knowing God. You may ask, "How did God know us before the foundation of the world?" Well, a good example is concerning Esau and Jacob. Malachi 1:2-3 KJV says—(2) *I have loved you, saith the Lord (Yahweh), yet you say, wherein hast thou loved us? Was not Esan Jacob's brother? saith the Lord (Yahweh): Yet I loved Jacob.* (3) *And I hated Esau, and laid his mountains and his heritage waste for the dragons (jackals) of the wilderness.* And Romans 9:13 KJV says—*As it is written, Jacob have I loved but Esau have I hated.* This is before they were even born. Then Romans 9:10–12 KJV says—(10) *And not only this; but when Rebecca also had conceived by one, even by our father Isaac;* (11) *For the children being not yet born, neither having done any good or evil, that the purpose of God according to election might stand, not of works but of him that calleth.* (12) *It was said onto her, the elder shall serve the younger.*

God loved (past tense) Jacob and hated (past tense) Esau before they were born. How can this be? This is why I believe that we existed then, before the foundation of the world, in spiritual bodies. He knew us then and chose us then. What we are in the flesh body now corresponds to what we were then in our spiritual bodies. Our physical appearance also takes after our spiritual appearance, which is why the disciples would recognize the Lord Jesus Christ after his death and resurrection, though he was not in the flesh body but in the spiritual body.

Psalms 139:13–16 says it very well—(13) *For thou hast possessed (created) my reins (inmost being): thou hast covered (woven) me in my mother's womb.* (14) *I will praise thee: for I am fearfully and wonderfully made (I am in awe); marvelously wonderful are thy work: and that my soul (myself) knoweth right well.* (15) *My substance (bone frame) was not hid from thee, when I was made in secret (in a secret place) and curiously wrought (intricately woven) in the lowest parts of the earth.* (16) *Thine eyes did see my substance (embryo), yet being unperfect (unfinished); and in thy book all my members (parts) were written, which in continuance were fashioned (in days they should be fashioned), when as yet there was none of them.*

And Psalms 139:6 says—*Such knowledge is too wonderful (too great) for me; it is high, I cannot attain unto it (prevail against it).* Indeed, it's too great a thing for me to fully comprehend.

Chapter 3:
The Three Heavens

God created the heavens and the earth that then was to inhabit his plan and purpose. The heavens (sky) were created to inhabit all the constellations, and above the constellations is the unseen spiritual world, which is the dwelling place of Satan, the devil, and his principalities, powers, and authorities. This is the kingdom of Satan, the devil, and above the kingdom of the devil is the tabernacle (the throne) of our Father, God almighty. For there are three heavens, the first one being the sky and the second one being the dwelling place of Satan, the devil, and the third one being the throne of God, the all-powerful. How can we establish this to be true? Well, the scripture is the only source of all truth. 2 Corinthians 12:2 says—*I knew (intuitively) a man in Christ above (before) fourteen years ago, whether in the body, I cannot tell (know); or whether out of (outside) the body, I cannot tell (I do not know): God knoweth; such a one (man) caught up (snatched) to the third heaven (singular).* (Verse 12:3 says—*And I knew (intuitively) such a man whether in the body or out of (outside) the body, I cannot tell (I do not know): God knoweth (knows).*

How is it that he was caught up (snatched away) to paradise (the paradise of God) and heard unspeakable (inexpressible by humans) words (rhema) that are not lawful (permitted) for a man to utter (talk)? The Apostle Paul describes his out-of-body experience, though he did not know that he was outside of his body because we know that flesh and blood cannot inherit the kingdom of God. He was snatched away to the third heaven, where the paradise of God is. And we know that the devil is in heaven too, but not the third heaven. After Satan's (Lucifer's) fall, he was cast down from the third heaven and he (Satan) was able to go back and forth between the earth and the second heaven, where he set his headquarters (his kingdom). But there will come a time when he, Satan, and his kingdom will be cast down to the earth, and I believe this will happen in this generation. We are that generation that shall see the end. I have so much to say about this and, God willing, I will do so as soon as God gives me the grace, because this needs to be heard: Romans 13:12—*The night is far spent, the day is at hand.*

Revelation 12:7–9 says—(7) *And there was (about to be) war in heaven (singular dwelling place of Satan and his angels—that is the kingdom of darkness). Michael (the archangel) and his angels fought against (went forth to war) the dragon, and the dragon fought and his angels, (8) and prevailed not (had no force), neither (not even) was their place found any more (henceforth) in heaven (singular). (9) And the great dragon was cast out (cast down; no place for him in heaven), that old serpent (the ancient serpent of Genesis 3:1) called the Devil (slanderer), and Satan (adversary) which deceiveth (the one deceiving) the whole world (the world as inhabited): he was cast out (cast down) into (on the) earth, and his angels were cast out (cast down) with him (the devil).* This is the second heaven, which is the dwelling place of the devil, Satan, and his angels for now, but they will be cast down very, very soon, and we shall live to see it in this generation.

The first heavens (plural) to contrast it with the earth are where all the constellations are, the sun, the moon, and all the stars. It is the visible heavens, therefore the sky. These heavenly bodies of mass were created and set forth in the heavens by God for the sole purpose to aid the earth and not to be inhabited by humans or to be worshipped. Genesis 1:14–19—(14) *And God said, let there be lights (luminaries) in the firmament (expanse) of the heaven to divide the day from the night, and let them be for signs (things to come), and for seasons (appointed times), and for days and years. (15) And let them be lights in the firmament (expanse or stretch) of the heavens to give light upon the earth, and it was so. (16) And God made two (the two) great lights, the greater light (the sun) to rule the day, and the lesser light (the moon) to rule the night; he made the stars also (for signs, therefore for something or someone to come).* These stars are named and numbered, and are signs of the zodiac but, as usual, man has turned what God meant for good into evil. (17) *And God set them in the firmament (expanse) of the heaven to give light upon the earth.* (18) *And to rule over the day and over the night and to divide the light from the darkness, and God saw that it was good.* (19) *And the evening and the morning were the fourth day.* So we see that God created the heavens and the earth both to be inhabited—the heavens to be inhabited by the constellations to aid the earth, and the earth to be inhabited by creatures. The heavens and the earth that then was, in Genesis 1:1, were inhabited to fulfill the purpose of God.

Isaiah 45:18 says—*For thus saith the Lord that created the heavens, God himself that formed the earth and made it, he hath established it, he created it not in vain, he formed it to be inhabited. I am the Lord and there is none else.* This is why I believe we existed then but in spirit bodies, and this earth that then was, was inhabited by creatures such as dinosaurs.

Job 40:15–24—(15) *Behold now behemoth, which I made with thee; he eateth grass as an ox. (16) Lo now, his strength is in his loins, and his force is in the navel of his belly. (17) He moveth his tail like a cedar; the sinews of his stones are wrapped together. (18) His bones are as strong pieces of brass; his bones are like bars of iron. (19) He is the chief of the ways of God; he that made him can make his sword to approach unto him.* (20) *Surely the mountains bring him forth food, where all the beasts of the field play.* (21) *He lieth under the shady trees, in the covert of the reed and fens.* (22) *The shady trees cover him with their shadow; the willows of the brook compass him about.* (23) *Behold, he drinketh up a river and hasteth not; he trusteth that he can draw up Jordan into his mouth.* (24) *He taketh it with his eyes, his nose pierceth through snares.*

Now many translators have said the behemoth is a hippopotamus, but hippopotamuses are aquatic and have a short tail. Yes, their diet consists entirely of grass, but they may also eat plants grown on the riverbanks. But the description of the behemoth here is a picture of an enormous land beast with a tail that moves like a cedar tree, so its tail is long and it gets its food by the mountainside, which means it eats both grass and leaves. For an animal to eat leaves, it has to be tall if it's a land animal, and it says that he lieth under the shady trees—only land animals seek shade under the trees. The hippo spends most of its time in the water. That's why I believe this to be a description of a dinosaur. These are the creatures of the earth that then inhabited the earth as created by God in Genesis 1:1, but God had to destroy all that was on earth by overflowing it with water, and that's why the dinosaurs are not part of this earth that is now. I will expound on this in the next chapter.

Chapter 4:
The Destruction of the
Then-World

I will pick up from where I left off in the last chapter to establish why God overflowed the world (cosmos) that then was. 2 Peter 3:6 says— ***Whereby (which means), the world (cosmos; the universe as a whole) that then was (existed at that time in Genesis 1:1), being overflowed with water (inundated or submerged), perished (destroyed utterly; not to extinction but to ruin, therefore loss of well-being).*** In Genesis 1:1 God created the heavens and the earth as good, perfect, and beautiful. Then why did God submerge it with water? And by the way, this was not the flood of Noah. To understand and comprehend this, we go again to the source of all truth: the scriptures.

Genesis 1:2 says—***And the earth was (became) without form and void (waste, empty and desolated); and darkness was upon (over) the face (surface) of the deep (abyss of the water) and the spirit of God moved upon the face (over the surface) of the water.*** These two scriptures give us a picture of how the world that then was, then created heavens and the earth of Genesis 1:1, which God created as perfect, were utterly destroyed by being submerged with water and became a ruin. Therefore, in Hebrew "TOHU VA BOHU" refers to waste, emptiness, and desolation, but not created "TOHU VA BOHU" became to be. So we are told how the perfect heavens and the earth became a ruin in 2 Peter 3:6 and a picture of the aftermath of a submerged and ruined heaven and earth that was in Genesis 1:2, and that the spirit of God moved swiftly over the surface of the deep water, therefore over the ruined heavens and the earth that then was what God created in Genesis 1:1. But we are not told what happened or what caused God to submerge and ruin the perfect world that he had created. To have a clear picture and understanding of the ruined world, let's search the scriptures.

Psalms 104:6—*Thou coveredst (covered) it (the world) with the deep (abyss of water) as with a garment; the waters stood above (over) the mountains.* And Job 38:30 says—*The waters are hid as with a stone, and the face (surface) of the deep (abyss of water) is frozen.* Literally, as turned to stone, the surface of the abyss of water froze and the water hid them. That's why there was darkness over the surface of the deep. Darkness represents ruin in the absence of the presence of God. And that's why the spirit of God moved swiftly over the surface of the deep to bring the presence of God. The spirit of God is the representation and the carrier of the presence of God and the carrier of the glory of God. Where the spirit is, there is the presence of God and the Son. The spirit cannot be where God the Father and God the Son are not. When the spirit of God moved over the surface of the frozen deep of the world that then was, it signified (marked) the beginning of the heavens and the earth that are now—2 Peter 3:7. Now, let's find out why God destroyed the heavens and the earth that then was—2 Peter 3:6, which is the created heavens and earth that are in Genesis 1:1. First of all, we don't know how long the heavens and the earth that then were, as created by God in Genesis 1:1, existed or how long it was kept in a ruined, frozen state, but we can assume that they existed millions or billions of years ago.

And we can also assume the same for how long they were kept in a frozen state from my studies on how God operates in dispensations or administrations of time. The numbers three and seven have been mightily used because three and seven are divine numbers to God. The number three is the number of divine perfection or completeness and has to do with the purpose of God. And the number seven is the number of spiritual perfection or completeness, and has to do with the council of God.

From what we can gather from scripture, there was a falling away or a departure from the divine will and divine purpose of God after Genesis 1:1 that caused God to destroy the then-created heavens and the earth and bring them to a ruined state. God is not a God of confusion or disorder. Ezekiel 28:12–18 gives us the reason why God brought a flood over the world that then was as created by God. (12) ***Son of man, take up a lamentation upon the king of Tyrus (Satan named as a type of prince that is to become the antichrist), and say unto him (Satan—a super terrestrial being), thus saith the Lord God; thou sealest up the sum (you are the finished pattern), full of wisdom, and perfect in beauty. (13) Thou hast been (was) in Eden, the garden of God; every precious stone was thy covering, the sardius, topaz, and the diamond, the beryl, the onyx, and the jasper, the sapphire, the emerald, and the carbuncle, and gold: the workmanship (craftsmanship) of thy tabrets and of thy pipes was prepared in thee (and gold was the craftsmanship of your settings and your mountings in you) in the day that thou wast created. (14) Thou art (was) the anointed cherub that covereth (an anointed cherub—a supernatural being that oversees and therefore protects the world that then was) and I have set thee so; thou wast upon the holy mountain of God; thou hast walked up and down (to and fro) in the midst of the stones of fire. (15) Thou wast (you were blameless) perfect (before his fall) in thy ways from the day that thou wast created, till iniquity (perversity, unjust and deceitful, that which is not equal and right, therefore unfairness in dealings hence craft) was found in thee. (16) By the multitude (abundance) of thy merchandise (trafficking or trading), they have filled (puffed you up in heart) the midst of thee with violence (malicious, hence the disruption*** *of the divinely established order of things), and thou hast sinned (you missed the mark, hence came short, therefore was found worthless); therefore, I will cast thee as profane (I will expose you as unholy) out of (from) the mountain of God (the holy place of God), and I will destroy thee (expel you) from (out of) the midst of the stones of fire.* (17) *Thine heart was lifted up (puffed up, therefore prideful) because of thy beauty, thou hast corrupted (did corrupt) thy wisdom by reason of thy brightness (splendor), I will cast you thee (I threw you down) to the ground (earth), I will lay thee (literally expose) before kings (in the face of kings), that they may behold thee (they would view you).* We are not told when this took place, but it happened before Genesis 3:1, and the only time this might have taken place is between Genesis 1:1 and Genesis 1:2. This is what caused God to flood the world that then was of Genesis 1:1 with water. Lucifer (the anointed cherub, Satan, the devil, the dragon, and the serpent) became puffed up in his heart because of his beauty and his abundance in trading, and became prideful, and by so doing, he corrupted and perverted all his ways and all he was put in charge of. God found his ways and dealings unrighteous. He went against the divine order and will of God. So God had to cast him down from his presence, and since he corrupted the divine order of things on the earth, God had to destroy the world that then was and bring ruin to the earth. (18) *Thou hast defiled (corrupted) thy sanctuary (sanctuary of deity) by the multitude (abundance) of thine iniquities (perversities), by the iniquity (deceitfulness) of thy traffick (trading). Therefore, I will bring forth a fire from the midst of thee (I profaned your sanctuary by bringing fire). It shall devour (consume) you and I will bring thee to ashes (I have turned you to ashes) upon the earth in the sight of all them that behold thee (before the eyes of everyone who sees you).*

God has already pronounced a sentence for the devil. Verse 18 gives us that judgment; death by fire, but this is yet in the future. Revelation 20:10—*And the devil that deceived them was cast into the lake of fire and brimstone, where the beast and the false prophet are, and shall be tormented day and night for ever and ever.* He is still in the heavens for a short time but will be cast down to the earth by the archangel Michael and his angels. Revelations 12:7—*Then war broke out in heaven. Michael and his angels fought against the dragon, and the dragon and his angels fought back.* And this will happen before the last seven years of tribulation. So from what we can gather from this scripture, the anointed cherub that covereth is Lucifer, and Lucifer is the serpent of Genesis 3:1.

Revelations 12:9 gives us all his names, and the great dragon was cast out (down). That (the) old (ancient) serpent—Genesis 3:1, called the devil (slanderer) and Satan (adversary) which deceiveth (the one deceiving) the whole world (inhabited world), he was cast out (down) into (on) the earth, and his angels were cast out (down) with him. But this verse is yet in the future, but very soon.

Cherubim, or "cherub" in the singular—are supernatural beings, angels of the highest order that God created. This first mention of a cherub in the Bible is in Genesis 3:24—*So he drove out the man and he placed at the east of the garden of Eden Cherubim and a flaming sword which turned every way, to keep the way of the tree of life.* Cherubim were placed to preserve the way of the tree of life so that the man, Adam, should not eat of it and live forever in his fallen state. So in the same way, the anointed cherub, Lucifer, was put in the then-inhabited world of Genesis 1:1 to preserve the divine ways of order of things ordained by God. But Lucifer defiled and corrupted the divine ways of order of things ordained by God because of his pride. And so God had to destroy the then-inhabited world of Genesis 1:1, the world that then was. 2 Peter 3:6—*Whereby, the world that then was being overflowed (submerged) with water, perished (utterly destroyed).* The anointed cherub, Lucifer, was filled with pride in his heart, and that was his downfall. Proverbs 11:2 says—*Pride comes, then disgrace comes, but wisdom is with the humble.* A lesson for all of us, what the spirit of pride can do.

But even when he was cast down from heaven, the mountain of God, Lucifer still believed in his heart that he could still ascend into heaven and be like God. Isaiah 14:12-15—*How art thou fallen from heaven, O*

Lucifer (a name morning of the Satan star), son of the morning (dawn)! How art thou cut down to the ground, which didst weaken (subdued) the nations! (13) *For thou hast said in thine heart, I will ascend (mount up) into heaven (the heavens, therefore the skies); I will exalt my throne above the stars (where his throne is at the moment) of God. I will sit also upon the mount of the congregation (assembly of judgement), in the sides of the north (the dwelling place of God).* (14) *I will ascend above the heights (the high place) of the clouds. I will be like the most High (the possessor of then heaven and earth, a title of God).* (15) *Yet thou shalt be brought down to hell (not the lake of fire but a holding place of the unrighteous), to the sides (depths) of the pit (abyss). This is yet in the future, but very soon.*

So now we know where Satan, the devil's throne, is: above the stars in the sides of the north—the north being the highest point in the sky where the throne of God is. Satan has set his throne between the sky and throne of God, therefore the second heaven. But there is coming a time when the archangel, Michael, and his angels will cast Satan and his angels down to the earth; yes, literally he will be physically on the earth—Revelation 12:7–9: (7) *And there was war in heaven. Michael and his angels fought against the dragon, and the dragon fought and his angels,* (8) *prevailed not. Neither was their place found any more in heaven.* (9) *And the great dragon was cast out, that old serpent, called the devil and Satan, which deceiveth the whole world; he was cast out into the earth, and his angels were cast out with him.*

To conclude this chapter, we have established that in the beginning (the initiation of the physical heavens and the earth), God created the heavens and the earth that then was perfect according to his divine will and order of things. But Lucifer, the anointed cherub, Satan, the devil got puffed up in his heart because of his beauty and abundance in trading, defiled and corrupted the divine order of things in his dealings, and thereby sinned against God. Since the world that then was, was entrusted to him, he got prideful and did things contrary to the divine order of the things of God, and by so doing, he corrupted all his ways. After being found deceitful, he was cast down from the throne of God, and because the divine order of things was perverted, God had to destroy the then-world by inundating it with water, and so it became submerged and there was a deep layer of water over the surface of the earth, and it became frozen.

CHAPTER 5:
THERE IS NONE ELSE!

Let's look at the heavens and the earth that are now. 2 Peter 3:7—***But the heavens and the earth, which are now, by the same word are kept in store (treasured up), reserved unto (for) fire against (unto) the day of judgement and perdition (destruction) of ungodly (impiety; absence of the fear of God and have no reverence for sacred things) men (people).***

We don't know how long the heavens and the earth that then were, as created by God in Genesis 1:1, were inundated with water, but by comparing scripture with scripture, we can establish the beginning of the heavens and the earth that are now. Genesis 1:2—***And the earth was without form and void (and the earth became waste, empty and desolate but not created waste and desolate but became so after being submerged with water and was destroyed), and darkness was (came to be) upon the face of the deep (over the surface of the abyss of water). And the Spirit of God moved upon the face of the waters (hovering above the surface of the abyss of water).*** Now, this is the beginning of the heavens and the earth that are now—2 Peter 3:7. The spirit of God moved above the surface of the frozen depths of water, causing darkness to flee. *And God said, let there be light and there was light* (Gen. 1:3).

This first thing that God (Elohim) did was to make his presence manifest. Where the spirit of God is, there is liberty, and where there is liberty, there is the Godhead—that is the Father, the Son, and the Spirit. This is the divinity of God, and where the divinity of God is, there is no darkness because darkness cannot comprehend the presence of God. *In him was life, and the life was the light of the world. And the light shineth in darkness, and the darkness comprehended it not* (John 1:4–5).

Then Jesus spoke to them again saying, I am the light of the world. The one who follows me will never walk in darkness, but will have the light of life (John 8:12).

Jesus Christ is the light of the world and the spirit is the bearer of the light. This light is the brightness of God, and it's not the same light in Genesis 1:14.

Let's look at the creation of the heavens and the earth that are now, and in the next chapters we will look at why God created the heavens and the earth, for Isaiah 45:18 says—*For thus saith the Lord that created the heavens, God himself that formed the earth and made it; he hath established it, he created it not in vain (waste and empty), he formed it to be inhabited: I am the Lord, and there is none else.* God is the absolute Creator of the heavens and the earth and all that is in the heavens and the earth. Both the invisible (celestial) and the visible (terrestrial), and He alone is the one and only true God—besides Him, there is none else (no one else).

In Genesis 1:2 the spirit of God moved, literally was hovering over the surface of the frozen earth, and this was the beginning of the heavens and the earth that are now. It is even so in us believers: First the spirit of God moves over us and darkness flees because darkness cannot subdue the light. And then after the light subdues the darkness, the spirit starts to regenerate us and make us into a new creation. *Therefore, if any man (person) be in Christ, he (or she) is a new creation. The old things have passed away. Behold, new things have come* (2 Cor. 5:17).

It is the same thing that happened in Genesis 1:2. He moved and started to regenerate the heavens and the earth that then were in Genesis 1:1. But at the same time, the regenerated heavens and earth, which are now, will be destroyed at the end of time, which is the end of the age, with fire. 2 Peter 3:7 says—*But the heavens and the earth, which are now, by the same word are kept in store, reserved unto fire against the day of judgement and perdition of ungodly men.* 2 Peter 3:10 says—*But the day of the Lord will come as a thief in the night, in which the heavens shall pass away with a great noise and the elements (substances) shall melt (dissolve) with fervent heat (being burned up), the earth also and the works that are therein (the deeds done in it) shall be burned up (consumed wholly by fire).* Brothers and sisters, these things are emphatic; they will happen.

Seeing then that all these things shall be dissolved, what manner of persons ought ye to be in holy conversation (behavior) and godliness (having the reverence for God) (2 Pet. 3:11). *Nevertheless, we, according to his promise, look for new (flesh) heavens and new (flesh) earth. Wherein dwelleth (resides) righteousness* (2 Pet. 3:13). *And I saw a new (flesh) heaven and a new (flesh) earth (the world as inhabited), for the first (former) heaven (heavens) and the first (former) earth were passed away, and there was no more sea* (Rev. 21:1). This first indicates this heaven and the earth that are now.

These things will happen, literally. That's why when God called on me, I became radical for his word. I cut myself off from everything that easily entangled me in the things of this world, and when I say *everything,* I mean everything, including people who were not supposed to be in my life. I cried unto God that He may teach me His word so that I may know Him and the person of Jesus Christ, and my life has never been the same.

He gave me grace to know and understand His word, and I started living by every word of God. That is why I ask and encourage every believer in Christ to do away with the things of this world and to live by every word that comes out of the mouth of God and live a life that's well pleasing to God. And to those who may not know Christ but, by the grace of God, may read this book to find Christ in their hearts and repent of their sins because the night is far gone, the day is at hand. I beg you, and I am not ashamed to beg, for I know what is about to come upon this earth.

Now let us take a look at how God regenerated the heavens and earth that are now—that *was* without form and void, and that became waste, empty and desolate. In the book of Genesis there are words that the spirit has used to describe the actions of God. In the creation of the heavens and earth that then were and the regeneration of the heavens and the earth that are now:

1. "God created" occurs six times in the introduction of Genesis 1:1, 21, 27, 27 again, and 27 yet again, and 2:3. The number six denotes the human number. For man (humankind) of Genesis 1:26, not the man Adam from Genesis 1:27, was created on the sixth day; I will expound on this later. The number six and its multiples are all connected to man; for example, man works six days and the hours of his days are multiples of six. It's the hallmark of defiance toward God, hence the number 6 is the marked number for the antichrist.

2. "God moved" occurs once in Genesis 1:2. The number one denotes unity or commencement.

3. "God said" occurs ten times: Genesis 1:3, 6, 9, 11, 14, 20, 24, 26, 28, and 29. The number ten denotes ordinal perfection, which is a number relating to order or rank—i.e., first and second—but in biblical terms means a new commencement, therefore a new first.

4. "God saw" occurs seven times: Genesis 1:4, 10, 12, 18, 21 18, 21, 25, and 31. The number seven denotes spiritual perfection or completeness. It's the number of the finished works of the spirit of God. The spirit of God regulates every dispensation or

administration of the determined works of God.

5. "God divided" occurs two times: Genesis 1:4 and 7. The number two denotes a difference in conclusiveness or division; for example, if two people agree on a thing, it is conclusive, but on the contrary, if they disagree on a thing, it's inconclusive. Therefore, division implies opposition and opposition brings enmity.

6. "God called" occurs five times: Genesis 1:5, again in 5, 8, 10, and again in 10. The number five denotes divine grace. It's God adding undeserved gifts and blessings to his creation.

7. "God made" occurs seven times: Genesis 1:7, 16, 25, 31, 2:2, again in 2, and 3. The number seven denotes spiritual perfection of completeness. Therefore, the number of finished works of the spirit of God to fulfill the divine will of God determined the order of things. The number seven is directly connected to the predetermined times; seasons, dispensations, and administrations of God's order of things.

8. "God set" occurs once in Genesis 1:17. The number one denotes commencement or unity.

9. "God blessed" occurs three times: Genesis 1:22, 28, and 2:3. The number three denotes divine completeness or perfection, and it implies the three days of the death and resurrection of the Lord Jesus Christ. Also, the number three represents the three world ages—the world that then was, the world that is now, and the new world that is yet to come. The number three includes also the resurrection of the earth out of the deep, and all vegetation rose from the ground.

10. "God ended" occurs once in Genesis 2:2, denoting the end of God's creativity works as a whole unity and making the commencement of God's creativity works in action.

11. "He (God) rested" occurs two times: Genesis 2:2 and 3. The number two denotes difference, therefore division between the days of creativity works and seventh day of rest. Now, God rested on the seventh day not because He was tired, but I believe He rested from His achievements that He had done and blessed the seventh day as the fulfillment of His divine will.

12. "He (God) sanctified" occurs once in Genesis 2:3. God sanctified the seventh day—that is, He marked it holy. The seventh day is the day after He finished His creativity works and the day before the commencement of His purpose pertaining to His creativity works. So the seventh day separates the creation and the purpose, but both the creation and the purpose work as a unity all to fulfill God's will.

There are two words that need to be contrasted to really understand their usage, and these two words are "created" and "made."

The word "created" implies something coming into being from without—that is, from nothing substantial that preexisted before. Therefore, God created the heavens and the earth from nothing substantial but by His word. He spoke the word and the heavens and the earth came into manifestation. I know that's mind-blowing, but who can comprehend the mind of God? No one. What we are given is what God has allowed us to know. Beyond that, only the spirit Himself can make us understand the hidden mysteries of God. He spoke it and by faith we believe and acknowledge that His word is the ultimate truth and that it has been tested and found to be absolute truth. That is why I love the word of God and I live by it, because it is life and life everlasting. Believe me, I testify to it and I confess it because it has changed my life. I have grown to know God, my Father, and to love my Lord Jesus Christ. He is the love of my soul.

The word "made" implies something coming into being from something substantial that preexisted before, therefore forming something from existing materials as it's used in Genesis 1:7, 26, and 27.

CHAPTER 6:
THE CREATION OF THE HEAVENS AND THE EARTH THAT ARE NOW

In this chapter we are going to look at how God (Elohim, the Creator) created and made the heavens and the earth that are now. 2 Peter 3:7—***But the heavens and the earth, which are now, by the same word are kept in store (treasured up), reserved unto (for) fire against (unto) the day of judgement and perdition (ruin or destruction) of ungodly men (impiety or absence of the fear of God and having no reverence of deity for God).***

In Genesis 1:3–5 God (Elohim, the Creator) did not create or make anything, but He was laying a foundation by making Himself present in the third person of His deity, the spirit. Where the spirit is, God the Father and God the son are present also; they are inseparable. God the Father, God the Son, and God the Spirit are one and make up the divinity of God. That's why in Hebrew, God the Creator is called Elohim (plural), the three persons of the Godhead. He established the beginning of time by separating the light from the darkness, and He called the light Day and the darkness Night, and called the day and night the first day. Therefore the day, according to God's establishment of time, starts at dawn, which is 6 a.m., and goes to dusk, which is 6 p.m., and the night starts at dusk, which is 6 p.m., and goes to dawn again, which is 6 a.m. It is a twelve-hour day and twelve-hour night, which adds up to twenty-four hours, and twenty-four hours makes a full/complete day. This is how the Jews count their days as established by God but, as usual, everything God established according to His will, His divine order of things, has been perverted by ungodly people. The count of a day was perverted to 12 a.m. to 12 p.m., and 12 p.m. to 12 a.m., which adds up to twenty-four hours, which makes up a full/complete day. God established the beginning of time in Genesis 1:2 and He established evenings to commence the night and mornings to commence the day, and that the evenings and the mornings make up a full/complete day in Genesis 1:5.

Now, let's look at how God created and made the heavens and earth that are now verse by verse, starting from Genesis 1:6—*And God (Elohim plural) said, Let there be a firmament in the midst of the waters, and let it divide the waters from the waters).* And God (Elohim plural, signifying God the Father, God the Son, and God the Spirit), meaning the three persons of the Godhead. A good example of how the Godhead works is found in 1 Corinthians 12:4–6. (4) *Now there are varieties of gifts, but the same Spirit.* (5) *And there are the varieties of ministries, but the same Lord.* (6) *And there are varieties of activities, but it is the same God who works all things in all people.* Outside of the Godhead are the angels who God created to carry out His will. There are different kinds of angels who carry out different types of duties.

In verse 6 we are told that God (Elohim) said, Let there be a firmament. Now, you may notice that there are some things that God created and made and, at the same time, there are some things He called forth that may imply that the things about which He said "Let there be" may have existed in the heavens and the earth that then were as created in Genesis 1:1 but were not destroyed by the deep of water. The word "firmament" means an expanse or a space that is stretched out and fixed between two parallel surfaces. Therefore, He separated the waters of the sky from the waters of the land, and He put an expanse between the two parallel stretched surfaces that are the land and the sky. This is why I believe the earth's surface is like a dinner plate; the edges of the earth are higher so that waters can never run over, and when God submerged the earth that then was (2 Pet. 3:5), He did it by covering the earth with the sky that consisted of water, among other things, and the waters of the sky flooded the earth and submerged it, causing a deep of water, and it became without form and void; that is, it became waste, empty and desolate, and every living thing that had a soul, and everything that was corrupted by Lucifer the devil, was utterly destroyed. Remember, God created the earth to be inhabited. Isaiah 45:18—*He formed to be inhabited.*

Genesis 1:7—*And God (Elohim) made the firmament (expanse) and divide (separated) the waters which were under the firmament (under the expanse that is the waters on the earth) from the waters which were above the firmament (above the expanse that is the waters of the sky), and it was so.*

Genesis 1:8—*And God called the firmament Heaven (the sky and, in Hebrew, it means "lofty," therefore above the ground).* This is the realm of God's storehouse of rain. Genesis 8:2—*The fountains also of the deep and the windows of heaven were stopped, and the rain from heaven was restrained.* Snow: Isaiah 55:10—*For as the rain cometh down, and the snow from heaven, and returneth not thither, but watereth the earth, and maketh it bring forth and bud, that it may give seed to the sower, and bread to the eater.* Hail: Josh 10:11—*And it came to pass, as they fled from before Israel, and were in the going down to Bethoron, that the Lord cast down great stones from heaven upon them unto Azekah, and they died; they were more which died with hailstones than they whom the children of Israel slew with the sword.* Brimstone and fire: Genesis 19:24—*Then the Lord rained upon Sodom and upon Gomorrah brimstone and fire from the Lord out of heaven.*

And above this storage house is the realm of the sun, the moon, and the stars. This is what is called the heavens and the earth, the created physical world that God created in Genesis 1:1, and is also the heavens and the earth that then were in 2 Peter 3:5–6, which God destroyed by submerging them with water and made them anew (Gen. 1:2–17), which are the heavens and the earth that are now (2 Pet. 3:7), of which God will also destroy by fire and will make them anew. Revelation 21:1—*And I saw a new heaven and a new earth, for the first heaven and the first earth were passed away, and there was no more sea.* Then above the realm of the sun, the moon, and the stars are the realm of the unseen (celestial), the second heaven. This is where it's believed to be the abode or dwelling of the devil, Satan himself, and a third of the angels that followed him after he was cast down from the heaven of heavens, which is the third heaven, the dwelling place of God and the Lord Jesus Christ and His angels. The second heaven is the kingdom of Satan, and the third heaven is the kingdom of God the Father and God the Son.

Genesis 1:9-10—(9) *And God said, Let the waters under the heaven (sky) be gathered together unto one place, and let the dry land appear, and it was so.* (10) *And God called the dry land Earth and the gathering together of the waters called the Seas, and God saw that it was good (beautiful).*

Let us compare other scriptures to get more of an understanding of how God submerged the world that then was: Psalms 104:6-9—(6) *Thou coverest it with the deep as with a garment; the waters stood above the mountains.* (7)—*At thy rebuke, they fled; at the voice of thy thunder, they hasted away (ran off).* (8)—*They go up (ascended) by the mountains; they go down (drawn through) by the valleys unto the place which thou hast founded (established) for them.* (9)—*Thou hast set a bound that they may not pass over, that they turn not again to cover the earth.* And Psalms 18:15 says—*Then the channels of waters were seen, and the foundations of the world (the habitable world) were discovered (discovered) at thy rebuke, O Lord (Yahweh), at the blast of the breath of thy nostrils (by the breath of the wind of your nose.* Psalm 104:6 confirms Genesis 1:2 that God (Elohim) covered the earth with a deep of water, thereby submerging it, and when the spirit of God moved over the surface of the deep, a transformation started to occur. He commanded the separation of the waters of the sky and the waters of the earth to rescind to the place He had established for them, and He set a boundary that they may not cross over, and the stream of the sea became visible, and the foundation of the inhabited world was uncovered.

Genesis 1:11–12—(11) *And God said, Let the earth bring forth grass, the herb yielding seed (let the ground produce green plants that will bear seed), and the fruit tree yielding fruit (bearing fruit) after (according to) his kind, whose seed is in itself (in which there is seed), upon the earth; and it was so.* (12)—*And the earth (the ground) brought forth grass, and herb yielding seed (green plants bearing seed) after (according to) his kind, and the tree yielding (bearing) fruit, whose seed was in itself (in which there was seed), after (according to) his kind; and God saw that it was good (beautiful).* First the herb, then seed and first tree, then fruit with seed in it.

Therefore God (Elohim) commanded that the ground sprout different kinds of green plants bearing seed, according to its kind, and that the seed be disseminated for continuation of life and different kinds of fruit trees bearing fruit with seed of its kind, and the seed be disseminated for continuation of life, both the green plants and the fruit trees, to provide food for animals and humans. On the third day, He called forth the vegetation, which had already been there in the world that then was, to sprout out of the ground. This is different from the planting of the garden in Genesis 2:8 because here, in Genesis 1:11–12, it's God (Elohim) in creation, and it was before the forming of humankind, but in Genesis 2:8, it's the Lord God (the covenant God, therefore Yahweh, God the Son) and the garden was planted after the forming of the man, Adam.

Genesis 1:14–19—(14) *And God (Elohim) said, Let there be lights (luminaries),*—therefore, not the same light of Genesis 1:3, which was the brightness of His presence that provided the light, but here in verse 14, He sets the physical lights in the sky; just like in the new Jerusalem, there will be no physical light because His presence will be the light.—*in the firmament (expanse) of the heaven (sky) to divide (distinguish) the day from the night and let them be for signs (things to come), and seasons (appointed times,) and for days and years. (15) And let them be for lights in the firmament (expanse) of the heaven (sky) to give light upon the earth; and it was so. (16) And God (Elohim) made two (the two) great lights; the greater light (the sun) to rule the day, and the lesser light (the moon) to rule the night; he made the stars also (stars for signs of appointed things to come). (17) And God set them in the firmament (expanse) of the heaven (sky) to give light upon the earth. (18) And to rule over the day and over the night, and to divide (separate) the light from the darkness; and God saw that it was good (beautiful). (19) And the evening and the morning were the fourth day (day four).*

Revelation 21:23 says—*And the city had no need of the sun, neither of the moon, to shine in it; for the glory of God did lighten (did shine) it, and the Lamb is the light lamp thereof.* So God made the light sources and set them up in heaven (the sky) considered as the first heaven that constitutes the clouds, the sun, the moon, and the stars as light (luminous) for the earth. Everything that is in the sky was made to sustain the earth's divine order of things and appointed events—the sun for the day and the moon for the night and the stars for signs for appointed events to come. There is only one sun and one moon, but there are probably billions of stars differing in size and brightness, and for different signs of things or events to come. The stars are named and numbered by God.

There are twelve stars used to symbolize the nation of Israel that represent the twelve sons of Jacob and also the twelve disciples—the number twelve being a symbol of governmental perfection.

Psalms 104:19–24 says—(19) *He appointed (made) the moon for seasons (appointed times); the sun knoweth (knows as a person) his going down (time for the sun to set). (20) Thou makest darkness, and it is night; wherein (when) all the beasts (wild animals) of the forest do creep forth (about). (21) The young lions roar after (for) their prey and seek their meat (food) from God (Elohim). (22) When the sun ariseth (rises), they gather themselves together, and lay (lie) them down in their dens. (23) Man (humankind) goeth (goes) forth (out) unto his work and to his labour until the evening. (24) O Lord (Yahweh), how manifold are thy works (how many are your works!) in wisdom hast thou made them all (all of them you have done in wisdom), the earth is full of thy riches (creatures).* Indeed, by God's wisdom (Jesus Christ) everything was created, and by God's knowledge, everything consists and exists together, and by God's understanding, everything functions according to the divine order of things created. God established time, days, seasons, and years. This is the divine calendar of God that He gave the Israelites to abide by after the exodus from Egypt.

Genesis 1:20–25—(20) *And God said, Let the waters bring forth abundantly the moving creature (let the waters surge with schools of living creatures) that hath life, and fowl (birds) that may fly above (over) the earth in the open firmament of heaven (across the face of the expanse of the sky). (21) And God created (from nothing) great whales (giant sea creatures), and every living creature (souls) that moveth, which the waters brought forth abundantly (with which the waters are bountiful), after their kind (according to its kind), and every winged fowl (bird) after his kind (according to its kind); and God saw that it was good (beautiful). (22) And God (Elohim) blessed (the first blessing) them, saying, Be fruitful, and multiply (to increase by procreation), and fill the waters in the seas, and let fowl (birds) multiply in (on) the earth. (23) And the evening (end of the day) and the morning (beginning of the day; therefore, evening and morning complete the whole day) were the fifth (number of grace) day. (24) And God said, Let the earth bring forth the living creature (souls that have the breath of life) after his kind (according to its kind), cattle (domesticated animals), and creeping thing (insects, rodents, reptiles usually considered unclean by the Jews), and beast (wild animals) of the earth after his kind (according to its kind);*

and it was so. (25) *And God made (formed) the beast (wild animals) of the earth after his kind (after its kind), and cattle (domesticated animals) after their kind, and every thing that creepeth upon (on) the earth after his kind (after its kind); and God saw that it was good (beautiful).* God made all these animals from dust of the ground and put souls in them. The words "living creature" mean having a soul—that is, every thing on earth that has the breath of life in it and is liable to die.

Genesis 2:19—*And out of the ground the Lord God (Yahweh God) formed every beast (animal) of the field and every fowl (bird) of the air (sky), and brought them (each) unto (to) Adam (the man Adam) to see what he would call them (it); and whatsoever Adam (the man Adam) called every living creature (living soul), that was the name (its name) thereof.* Therefore, every living being that has the breath of life, including humankind, God formed from the ground (soil). And we know that there are different kinds of soil with different colors and textures, and this got me thinking! Did God form every race from different kinds and colors of the soil? If this is true, then that explains why we, as humankind, have different color tones and textures of the skin. But who has ever known the mind of God? No one. But what we are told is that everything that God created (from nothing) and made (formed from something) was very good (beautiful). That's why racism is a sin, because we are all made in the image and likeness of God. Racism is an evil spirit that causes divisions among all races and turns them against each other. It is the plan of the devil to separate us, and it's directly connected to the spirit of pride, thinking or putting oneself more highly than another. I caution all of us who call ourselves Christians, or profess to be Christians, to really look inside ourselves—and if by any means we put or think highly of ourselves because of our race, to repent because it's not of God. God is not a God of disorder but of order, love, and peace. Everything God created and made was very beautiful according to His will, so we are all beautiful in the body of Christ (as Christians) and should love one another and live in peace with each other despite where we came from or the color of our skin, as an example to the world. We are as individual representatives of

Christ Jesus, and we are the light of the world because the light of the world, Jesus Christ, lives in us and we live in Him, to the praise and glory of His holy name.

Genesis 1:26—*And God (Elohim) said, "Let us (the Godhead) make (form) man ("no article," [as in Hebrew; make versus create] here for mankind) in (as) our image (figure), after (according to) our likeness (outward resemblance); and let them have dominion (rule) over the fish of the sea, and over the fowl (birds) of the air (sky), and over the cattle (domesticated animals), and over all the earth (land) and over every creeping thing (insects, rodents and reptiles) that creepeth (swiftly moving) upon (on) the earth (the ground and in the air).* God's divine purpose to form mankind, as in a physical form, to represent His resemblance that is an outward appearance and not His attributes, implying God the Father spoke to God the Son and God the Spirit to form a patterned image of Himself to represent Himself on the earth as rulers of His divine creation—we were created to rule and to tend to God's creation. So humankind is patterned according to God's substance (bodily attributes) and not His essence (spiritual attributes), though we are to live by His essence—that is, His spiritual attributes—through His son, Jesus Christ, who is the mark of His substance and essence. Only the Lord Jesus Christ possessed both God's substance and God's essence bodily because He is the fullness of God and the expression of His image.

Colossians 1:15 says—*Who is the image of the invisible God, the firstborn of every creature (over all creation).* And Hebrews 1:3 says—*Who being the brightness of his glory, and the express image of his person (literally the exact copy of his substance), and upholding all things by the word of his power, when he had by himself purged our sins, sat down on the right hand of the Majesty on high.* Though the human body is patterned to resemble God's image bodily, the body has no expediency of whom God is because the flesh body only knows or rather is connected to the things earthly. Therefore, the body is just a house we live in. 1 Corinthians 6:19—*What? Know ye not that your body is the temple of the Holy Ghost which is in you, which ye have of God, and ye are not your own?*

Who we are is a spirit and a soul. The spirit gives consciousness to the soul and it becomes a living being. The body's actions reflect what our hearts and minds dictate. The mind gathers information by what we see and what we hear. The mind is the steering wheel of the body. What we do with the information our minds gather dictates our actions. The mind and the body are intertwined and conform to the things of this world. Romans 8:7—*Because the carnal mind is enmity against God; for it is not subject to the law of God, neither indeed can be.* Because the mindset of the flesh is enmity to God, for it is not subjected to the law of God, for it is not able to do so. The only connection between God and humans is through the inbreathed spirit imparted in us by God, which makes the soul become a living being, and it's through this spirit that we receive and acquire knowledge intuitively without recourse to conscious reasoning. It's through this acquired knowledge that we know intuitively that there is a higher power than us and that higher power is God. The information that is acquired through the inbreathed spirit is then submitted to the soul, and in turn, the soul submits the information to our human mind, and therefore our mind can either accept or reject the information. Faith comes by hearing, so it's what we do with the information we are given that determines who we become. We all know that most things we see that God created are beyond our understanding, but what we hear is meant for us to understand. That's why there are many faiths in the world and each faith is based on the information that we have received from the source of our belief. But we as Christians receive the living, divinely imparted word, which is spiritual in nature, and the source is God the Creator. He spoke the word and it was so, and by faith we believe it to be from God and that it's the ultimate truth. Therefore, God formed humankind according to His will and purpose in His own likeness; hence, all the races are God's workmanship.

Genesis 1:27—*So God created man (with the "article," in Hebrew tongue) in his own image, in the image of God created he him; male*

and female created he them. So when God did create (in His purpose), He created man, hence the man Adam with the article. Therefore, this man, Adam, is different from the man without the article mentioned in verse 26 who is in general humankind; that is, all races on the earth. That's why the word "created" is used for the man, Adam, to differentiate him from the man (humankind) made in verse 26. The purpose here is indicated, but the description of the act is in Genesis 2:7, 21–24—(7) ***And the Lord God formed man of the dust of the ground, and breathed into his nostrils the breath of life; and man became a living soul.*** (21) ***And the Lord God caused a deep sleep to fall upon Adam, and he slept: and he took one of his ribs, and closed up the flesh thereof;*** (22) ***And the rib, which the Lord God had taken from the man, made he a woman, and brought her unto the man.*** (23) ***And Adam said, This is now bone of my bones, and flesh of my flesh; she shall be call Woman, because she was taken out of Man.*** (24) ***Therefore, shall a man leave his father and his mother, and shall cleave unto his wife; and they shall be one flesh.*** And He, God, created them male and female implying (intending) them to be Adam and Eve. 1 Corinthians 11:8 says—***For the man is not of the woman; but the woman of the man.*** And the actual forming of Eve is in Genesis 2:20–23, which says—(20) ***And Adam gave names to all cattle, and to the fowl of the air and to every beast of the field; but for Adam there was not found an help meet (a help mate) for him.*** One important thing we have to understand is that from Genesis 2, the focus, or emphasis, is on this same man, Adam, because through the man Adam, God was to rule over His divine creation on the earth. This same man Adam was created and formed to carry out God's will on the earth, and God's purpose of creation was to begin through the man Adam. That's why Adam is called the first Adam, and the Lord Jesus Christ is called the second Adam. 1 Corinthians 15:45 says—***And so it is written, The first man Adam was made (became) a living soul (man); the last Adam was made (into) a quickening spirit (living resurrected body, therefore a spiritual body).*** But after his fall in the Garden of Eden, he relinquished his authority and rule over every living created thing on the earth to Lucifer, the serpent, the devil, and Satan. That's why God sent his only begotten son, Jesus Christ the Lord, the last Adam, to take back the authority and rule over every living created thing by defeating the devil through His death and resurrection. Now this is not yet fully fulfilled but will be at His second coming.

Genesis 1:28—*And God blessed them, and God said unto them, Be fruitful, and multiply, and replenish the earth, and subdue it; and have dominion over the fish of the sea, and over the fowl of the air, and over every living thing that moveth upon the earth.* And God blessed them— that is, Adam and Eve—for their continual dependence on God to exist and function. And God said to them (Adam and Eve), be fruitful and increase, and fill the earth and rule over it, and have jurisdiction over literally every living thing that has the breath of life in it on the earth. God made us to be above every living thing because we, as humans, are the only ones made in His image and/or likeness.

Genesis 1:29—*And God said , Behold (look), I have given you every herb (plant) bearing seed, which is upon the face (surface) of all the earth, and every tree, in the which is the fruit of a tree yielding seed (seeding seed); to you it shall be for meat (food).*

Genesis 1:30—*And to every beast (kind of animal) of the earth, and every fowl (bird) of the air, and to every thing that creepeth (moves swiftly) upon (on) the earth (ground), wherein there is life (soul), I have given every green herb (plant) for meat (food); and it was so.*

Genesis 1:31—*And God saw every thing that he had made (as a potter), and, behold (look), it was very good (very beautiful). And the evening and the morning were the sixth day (the sixth day with "article" [Hebrew meaning] unlike the other five days).*

CHAPTER 7:
THE FAMILY HISTORY OF THE HEAVENS AND THE EARTH

Genesis 2:1–3—(1) ***Thus the heavens and the earth were finished, and all the host of them. (2) And on the seventh day God ended his work which he had made; and he rested on the seventh day from all his work which he had made. (3) And God blessed the seventh day, and sanctified it: because that in it he had rested from all his work which God created and made.*** Now the heavens and the earth were finished—that is, the heavens (sky) and the earth that are now (2 Pet. 3:7), and all its arranged substance, hence, the heavens and all its contents: the clouds, the sun, the moon, and the stars. And the earth and all its contents: the waters and all kinds of fish in them, the ground with all kinds of plants and trees on it, and all kinds of animals, and all of humanity. This is the present world we live in that God created in Genesis 1:1 but destroyed by submerging it with water, and then made anew in Genesis 1:2, and He finished making it on the sixth day, not on the seventh day as written. He rested on the seventh day, not from fatigue but from what He had predetermined to accomplish. He foreknew His plan and purpose before He created it—that's the foreknowledge of the all-knowing God. He blessed and sanctified it—that is, He set it apart and blessed it for a continual existence and function, and made it holy. Therefore, He separated the seventh day from the six days of work for Himself, to be glorified and worshipped. There are only three blessings mentioned in creation; two involve and include all living creatures that have breath of life in them, but He did not sanctify them. God only blesses something that has His approval and renders His virtue and makes holy that which is sacred to Him. God's blessings avail much, even when people do not approve, and set aside what is sacred. Only God is holy in all His ways, and that's why when God sanctifies you, He sets you apart for His purpose that He has predetermined for you.

Genesis 2:4—*These are the generations of the heavens and of the earth when they were created, in the day that the Lord God made the earth and the heavens.* "These are the generations" literally means the family history or record of the heavens and the earth when they were created—that is the heavens and earth that were then (2 Pet. 3:6), as created in Genesis 1:1. And the day the Lord (Yahweh) God made the earth and the heavens that are now (2 Pet. 3:7), as made in Genesis 1:2 after the heavens and the earth that were then were destroyed by God.

There are fourteen generations in the Bible, of which eleven are in the book of Genesis and one is in the book of Numbers 3:1, that of Moses and Aaron, and the other one is in the book of Ruth 4:18–22, that of Pharez, and the last one is in the book of Matthew 1:1, that of the Lord Jesus Christ. So thirteen are in the Old Testament and one is in the New Testament. The one thing to note is that from Genesis 2, the title God (Elohim) changes to the Lord God (Yahweh God). That's the covenant God is in relationship to His creation and, more importantly, to His chosen ones. The Jews began from the man Adam, in whom Yahweh God would enact his plan and purpose, and, from the man Adam, through Seth, Noah, Abram, Isaac, Jacob, all the way to the Lord Jesus Christ.

Genesis 2:5–6 says—(5) ***And every plant of the field (open land) before it was in the earth (ground), and every herb (plant) of the field (open land) before it grew (sprung): for (reason) the Lord (Yahweh) God had not caused it to rain upon the earth (land), and there was not a man to till (cultivate) the ground.*** The reason why Yahweh God caused it not to rain is because there was not a man—that is, the man Adam who was to cultivate the ground and keep it, as stated in Genesis 2:15—***And the Lord God took the man, and put him into the Garden of Eden to dress it and to keep it.*** (6) ***But (before this same man, Adam, was formed), a mist went up from the ground to water the surface of the land.*** Yahweh God specifically chooses this land to put the man Adam on to cultivate and keep it after He has planted a garden—the Garden of Eden.

Genesis 2:7—***And the Lord (Yahweh) God formed man of the dust of the ground, and breathed into his nostrils the breath of life; and man became a living soul.*** We are here given more detailed information on how Yahweh God formed, as a potter, humankind (Genesis 1:26, and the man Adam of Genesis 1:27, also implied in Genesis 2:7). There is a difference between the man purposed in Genesis 1:26 and the man purposed in Genesis 1:27. The difference is in the meaning of the word "man," as used in Genesis 1:26, which has no article (Adam in Hebrew tongue); therefore it generally means all races or, if you will, all humankind. But the word "man" used in Genesis 1:27 and Genesis 2:5–7 has the article in the Hebrew tongue—Eth-Ha-Adham—meaning this same man Adam, therefore a specific man and of a specific race, different from those of Genesis 1:26. So through this same man Adam would come a peculiar people, the chosen ones of God, the Jews. God would carry on his plan and purpose on the earth through the same man, Adam.

God formed (as a potter) so as to mold or fashion in a desired shape. God fashioned humankind in his likeness as an image of his representation on the earth—that is, physically but not morally, because man failed the morality test. After the Lord (Yahweh) God formed this same man Adam from the dust, therefore soil of the ground, he breathed in his nostrils the breath of life that is, in Hebrew tongue, "neshamah," meaning the breath that is life, and this same man Adam became a living soul ("nephesh" in the Hebrew tongue, meaning a live person). Isaiah 64:8 says—***But now, O Lord (Yahweh) thou art our father; we are the clay, and thou our potter; and we all are the work of thy hand.*** Genesis 2:8—***And the Lord (Yahweh) God planted a garden eastward in Eden; and there he put the man (the man Adam) whom he had formed.*** This is a special garden planted (by Yahweh God) in a special field of land with specific plants for a specific person, the man Adam. The field is described in Ecclesiastes 2:5—***I made me gardens and orchards, and I planted trees in them of all kind of fruits.*** This place called Eden, the paradise of God, for which the Garden of Eden was lost after the man Adam and his wife, Eve, sinned. But we know that the Garden of Eden, which is the paradise of God, exists now in the third heaven. Revelation 2:7 says—***He that hath an ear, let him hear what the Spirit saith unto the churches; to him that overcometh will I give to eat of the tree of life, which is in the midst of the paradise of God.*** And we know, according to the Apostle Paul, it exists in the third heaven. 2 Corinthians 12:2 says—***I knew a man in Christ above (before) fourteen years ago, (whether in the body, I cannot tell; or whether out of the body, I cannot tell: God knoweth;) such an one caught up (snatched up) to the third heaven.*** And 2 Corinthians 12:4 says—***How that he was caught up (snatched up) into paradise, and heard unspeakable (inexpressible) words, which it is not lawful for a man to utter (say).***

Genesis 2:9—***And out of the ground made the Lord (Yahweh) God to grow every tree that is pleasant to the sight, and good for food; the tree of life also in the midst of the garden and tree of knowledge of good and evil.*** Yahweh God caused every tree to exist that is delightful to the eyes and its fruit desirable to be eaten. Yahweh God also put the tree of life that is to support the continuation of life that has been imparted. This tree of life is symbolic of the Lord Jesus Christ in whom we have everlasting life, the bread of life. This is the word that gives life, and He is also the source of the water of life. John 6:48 says—***I am that bread of life.*** And John 4:14 says—***But whosoever drinketh of the water that I shall give*** *him shall never thirst; but the water that I shall give him shall be in him a well of water springing up into everlasting life.*

The tree of knowledge (of good and evil) gives perception to know good and evil. By knowing good and evil, a person now has a choice of how he or she wants to live his or her life. So by eating the fruit of this tree, man now has a choice to perceive and determine what is good and what is evil. Since through this same man Adam the Yahweh God purposed his plans for all humanity, but he sinned, and since he sinned, we are all born sinners, which is why God had to send His son, Jesus Christ, the second Adam, so that through Him we might receive forgiveness of sins and receive salvation. What we choose, we become. Lucifer, the serpent, was the first to go against God's divine will and order of things.

Genesis 2:15—*And the Lord (Yahweh) God took the man, and put him into the Garden of Eden to dress it and to keep it.* One difference to note here is that God (Elohim) formed the man of Genesis 1:26—as the humankind that is all races—last, after he had created and made all other animals, plants, and fish, and the reason might be that God didn't want man to take any credit in creation. But when it came to forming the man Adam, implied in Genesis 1:27 and Genesis 2:7, the Lord (Yahweh) God that is the covenant God, and not God (Elohim) that is the Creator, formed the man Adam first before he planted a garden and made to grow every tree and put a river to flow from the garden in Eden. So God (Elohim) the Creator made all races implied in Genesis 1:26, but the Lord (Yahweh) God, the covenant God, made the man implied in Genesis 1:27 and Genesis 2:7 a different race, through which he would rule all other races that God (Elohim) made, implied in Genesis 1:26. Through this same man Adam would come the savior Christ Jesus. God (Elohim) was to bring all the races to Himself through the man Adam. That was His plan then through the first Adam, but he fell and sinned, and it is still His plan now through the second Adam, the Lord Jesus Christ, who is a descendant of the first Adam. In Him there was no sin, but He took on our sinful nature from the first Adam and became our sin sacrifice in order to bring all races back to

God the Creator as He had intended from the beginning. This Garden of Eden was a sanctuary for the righteous. The first Adam was made in the righteousness of God, but he lost God's righteousness when he sinned and that's why Lord (Yahweh) God took him out of the sanctuary of the righteous that is the paradise of God, which is now in heaven.

Genesis 2:16–17—(16) *And the Lord (Yahweh) God commanded the man, saying, Of every tree of the garden thou mayest freely eat:* (17) *But of the tree of the knowledge of good and evil, thou shalt not eat of it; for in the day that thou eatest thereof thou shalt surely die.* Yahweh God commanded;—the word "commanded" carries a connotation of a rule that a subordinate is to act in a recurring similar situation. Therefore, Yahweh God set forth the rules to the man Adam, not on conduct but on what he can eat and he cannot eat; this was the first occurrence of this word and the first occurrence of Yahweh God speaking to the man Adam. So just as every commandment has a blessing if you abide by it and a curse if you don't, and the blessing is life, the curse is death, and a provision has been given for everlasting life. By eating from the tree of life, the man Adam was to live forever. Now whether the man Adam ate from it (the tree of life) before he sinned because it was there in the midst of the garden, we are not told, but I assume he did. That's why Yahweh God had to take him out.

Adam was told to eat bountifully from every tree in the garden, including an apple tree. But Yahweh God commanded the man Adam not to eat from the tree of knowledge of good and evil, which is symbolically and figuratively expressed as the serpent Satan, the devil, just as the tree of life is expressed symbolically and figuratively for Christ Jesus. Just as also John 4:14—the water of life—*But whosoever drinketh of the water that I shall give him shall never thirst; but the water that I shall give him shall be in him a well of water springing up into everlasting life.* And John 6:48—*I am the bread of life.* And also John 6:55—*For my flesh is food indeed, and my blood is drink indeed.* These two terms are a figure of speech—the tree of life is literally Jesus Christ, and the tree of knowledge of good and evil is literally the devil. God put both of them in the garden to see who the man Adam would pick to live by. It was a test for the man Adam to make a choice between Christ and the devil, just as it still is a test for all humanity to choose between Christ and the devil. The term "to eat from it" literally means to be a partaker or a participant of anything that springs out of the devil. So when Eve was deceived by the serpent, the devil, she mentally and physically participated in his deception, and then she partook in his deception, and physically also gave it to her husband, the man Adam, to partake of. Yes, it truly happened, and it has nothing to do with an apple—more on this as we go on. Yahweh God tells the man Adam that if he partakes from the works of the devil, he shall surely die; He is emphatic that is a physical death.

Genesis 2:18—*And the Lord (Yahweh) God said, It is not good that the man (Adam) should be alone; I will make (for) him and help meet for him (a helpmate, as his counterpart, a helper as his equal).* Yahweh God made Eve for the man Adam to be his helper, as equal to him in the likeness of the man Adam. Eve was not made in the likeness of God but in the likeness of the man Adam, both in appearance and function, because she was taken from the man Adam, and that's why she is called a weaker visual. Yahweh God made Eve for the man Adam, not because he was lonely but because he was alone—to fulfill God's purpose.

Genesis 2:19–20—(19) *And out of the ground the Lord (Yahweh) God formed every beast (animals) of the field, and every fowl (birds) of the air; and brought them unto Adam to see what he would call them: and whatsoever Adam called every living creature (soul), that was the name thereof. (20) And Adam gave names to all cattle (domesticated animals), and to the fowl (birds) of the air, and to every beast (wild animal) of the field; but for (the man) Adam there was not found an help meet (a helper as his counterpart) for him.* This gives us more details on Genesis 1:24–25.

Genesis 2:21–23—(21) *And the Lord (Yahweh) God caused a deep sleep to fall upon Adam, and he slept; and he took one of his ribs, and closed up the flesh instead thereof (in its place); (22) And the rib, which the Lord God had taken from man, made he a woman, and brought her unto the man.* (23) *And Adam said, This is now bone of my bones and flesh of my flesh; she shall be called Woman, because she was taken out of Man.* Yahweh God made the man Adam to fall into a deep sleep, and He cut the side of the man Adam and took a curve out of the side of the man Adam, the side being the hip. The curve that Yahweh God took contained all the female organs, and He formed Eve's body from the dust of the ground, and He put the curve into the body of Eve and breathed into her nostrils the breath of life, and Eve became a living soul. The word "rib" implies a curved side and not the actual rib. If truly Yahweh God took a rib from the man Adam's rib cage, all men would have been short a rib, and that's a deficiency. God is not a God of disorder.

God created the first men of all races, and the first men had both male and female organs. He took the female organs and formed women's bodies of all races, and He put the female organs into the women's bodies. All races were created by God; no race came from the other, and yes, because of intermarriages between races, we have mixed races. Despite the color of our skin, we are all God's children and we are all created equal. God is not a respecter of persons—He does not look at the color of our skin but at our hearts. And He doesn't favor us because of our skin color, but He favors those who seek him diligently. We do not choose where we are born or the color of our skin, or who our parents should be. Yes, though we may be disadvantaged or advantaged by where we are born and by who our parents are, it is all about the will of God and always will be. This is why women have a more curved body than men. God did not make all races from the man Adam but made a man first of each race, and from each man, God made a woman, and that was the beginning of humanity on the earth, each race with its origin and region.

Genesis 2:24—*Therefore shall a man leave his father and his mother, and shall cleave (cling) unto (to) his wife; and they shall be one flesh.* The word "cleave," as used here in Hebrew, means "to cling," and it carries a connotation of one object of a person being joined to the other person's object; that is, as when a man and a woman are having intercourse, they become one flesh. This proves my point that God took the female parts from the man because when a man and a woman are having intercourse, the female parts are joined back to the man's body, and by doing so they become one flesh. This is why it's very important, as a born-again Christian, to wait upon the Lord to give you the right man or woman to be your partner, and by *partner* I don't mean man with man or woman with woman, which is perversion. The deviant world has perverted the meaning of marriage as God instituted it to be—a man and a woman. Marriage is a partnership between a man and a woman to fulfill the plan, purpose, and will of God, and anything outside the will of God is not of God. Homosexuality is not of God and it is therefore impossible to be a born-again Christian if you are homosexual or practice homosexuality; it is morally wrong and an abomination to God. 1 Corinthians 6:16 says—***Or do you not know that he who joins himself to a prostitute becomes one body with her? For as it is written, the two will become one flesh (body).*** If I knew then what I know now, I would have made good decisions with what I did with my body, but thanks be to God the Father for sending His only begotten son to be our sin offering. Through His blood I am cleansed; my body is no longer mine but the Lord's—my body for the Lord and the Lord for my body.

Genesis 2:25—***And they were both naked, the man and his wife, and were not ashamed.*** They were naked and were not ashamed because they only knew good and their minds were blocked from evil until their eyes were opened by the deception of the serpent, Satan, the devil. The word "ashamed" carries a connotation of disappointment after detecting a reproach.

CHAPTER 8:
THE CUNNINGNESS OF THE SERPENT, SATAN, THE DEVIL

Genesis 3:1—*Now the serpent was more subtil (cunning or crafty) than any beast (living creature) of the field which the Lord God had made. And he said unto the woman, Yea, hath God said, Ye shall not eat of every tree of the garden?* The phrase "rendered serpent" is a figure of speech. A figure of speech makes figurative what is literal, hence calling attention to, emphasizing, and intensifying the reality of the literal sense and truth conveyed by it. Although the words used might not be strictly true, it's more to enlighten the truth in the message conveyed. The Hebrew phrase "rendered serpent" is "*nachash*," meaning "to shine," therefore "the shining one"; just like in Chaldea, a Babylonian language, it means brass or copper because of its shiny appearance. To really understand who or what this serpent is, we go to the source of truth, the word of God.

Revelation 20:2 says—*And he laid hold on the dragon, that old serpent, which is the devil, and Satan, and bound him a thousand years.* This scripture gives us an overview of who or what the serpent is. He is called by other names but is the same entity, a supernatural being. He is called the dragon because of his keen power of sight, and he is called old serpent because of his deception in Revelation 20:2. He is called the ancient one to connect him to the serpent of Genesis 3:1 and to bring to light that the serpent of Genesis 3:1 is the same old serpent of Revelation 20:2 and the same one implied in Revelation 12:3—*And there appeared another wonder in heaven; and behold a great red dragon, having seven heads and ten horns, and seven crowns upon his heads.* He is called the devil because he is the accuser and slanderer, and he is called Satan because he is the adversary. He is also called the tempter who tempted the Lord Jesus Christ in Matthew 4:1—*Then was Jesus led up of the Spirit into the wilderness to be tempted of the devil.* He is the one who beguiled Eve in 2 Corinthians 11:3—*But I fear, lest by any means, as the serpent beguiled Eve through his subtilty, so your minds should be corrupted from the simplicity that is in Christ.* He is also spoken of as an angel of light in 2 Corinthians 11:4—*For if he that cometh preacheth another Jesus, whom we have not preached, or if ye receive another spirit, which ye have not received, or another gospel, which ye have not accepted, ye might well bear with him.* And he is called Lucifer in Ezekiel 28:11–19— (11) *Moreover the word of the Lord came unto me, saying,* (12) *Son of man, take up a lamentation upon the king of Tyrus (the name of Satan), and say unto him, Thus saith the Lord (Yahweh) God; thou sealest up the sum (you were a perfect model or pattern), full of wisdom, and perfect in beauty.* (13) *Thou hast been (were) in Eden the garden of God (Eholim); every precious stone was thy covering (adornment), the sardius, topaz, and the diamond, the beryl, the onyx, and the jasper, the sapphire, the emerald, and the carbuncle, and gold: the workmanship of thy tabrets and of thy pipes was prepared in thee in the day that thou wast created (and gold was the craftsmanship of your settings and your mountains in you on the day you were created, they were prepared).*

Here we are told that Satan, the serpent, was in the Garden of Eden, the garden of God (Elohim), where he is symbolically the tree of knowledge of good and evil, which is the tree that possesses wisdom to know good and evil. The tree refers to the frame of his body and the fruits refer to the parts of his body, and one of these parts, when having eaten the fruit, makes one wise to perceive that which is good and that which is evil, giving one power to decide within oneself what is good and what is evil in deciding your own ways, thereby putting God aside. He is figuratively the shining one—the serpent—because of his beauty adorned with all these precious ornaments; no wonder Eve was fascinated by his looks. God created him as a perfect model, one full of wisdom and perfect in beauty. (14) *Thou art the anointed cherub (supernatural being) that covereth (guardian); and I have set (placed) thee so: thou wast upon the holy mountain of God (literally I placed you on the mountain of the holiness of God); thou hast walked up and down (to and from) in the midst of the stones of fire.* (15) *Thou wast (were) perfect in thy ways from the day that thou wast created, till iniquity was found in thee.* Satan was blameless in his ways before he fell. (16) *By the multitude of thy merchandise (in the abundance of your trading) they have filled the midst of thee with violence (maliciousness), and thou hast sinned (did sin); therefore, I will cast thee as profane (not holy) out of the mountain of God (the mountain of the holiness of God), and I will destroy thee (expel you), O covering cherub (guardian), from the midst of the stones of fire.*

Lucifer, the guardian cherub, was anointed and appointed to overshadow and oversee the divine order of things of the world that then was in 2 Peter 3:6. And because of his abundance of authority and beauty, he was filled with pride and became malicious and, by so doing, profaned or corrupted and disrupted the divinely established order of things by God. Therefore, God found him unholy and cast him down from His presence, which is His throne in the third heaven. This is what led God to destroy the world that then was in 2 Peter 3:6. (17) *Thine heart was lifted up because of thy beauty, thou hast corrupted (did corrupt) thy wisdom (understanding) by reason of thy brightness (splendor); I will cast (throw) thee to the ground (earth), I will lay thee before (in the face of) kings, that thy may behold thee.* (18) *Thou hast defiled (profaned) thy sanctuaries by the multitude (abundance) of thine iniquities (perverseness or crookedness), by the iniquity (crookedness) of thy traffick (trading); therefore, I will bring forth a fire from the midst of thee, it shall devour (consume) thee, and I will bring thee to ashes upon the earth in the sight of all them that behold thee.* This will literally happen according to Revelation 20:10, which says—*And the devil that deceived them was cast into the lake of fire and brimstone, where the beast and the false prophet are, and shall be tormented day and night for ever after.*

We have now established who the serpent is and that he is not a literal snake but a supernatural being, a cherub, created by God for good and not for evil, but pride was found in him and evil took him over. By comparing scripture with scripture, we will have a clear understanding of the events that follow. 19) *All they that know thee among the people shall be astonished at thee; thou shalt be a terror, and never shalt thou be any more.* This is the same supernatural being but with different personalities and with one goal in his mind: to undermine God and to stop the will of God by first subverting the word of God, using the word of God with a twist to deceive people. He subverted the word of God in the Garden of Eden, and he twisted the word of God to tempt the Lord Jesus Christ in the wilderness. He has not changed his tactics and he will always use the word of God as a front to deceive people, even we who are born again, if we allow him. Unfortunately, he has taken over most of the churches, using the church as a cover to fulfill his craftiness. He is Lucifer, a mighty angel, a cherub, Satan, the devil. Isaiah 14:12–15 says it about him in this way—(12) *How art thou fallen from heaven, O Lucifer (morning star), son of the morning (son of the dawn)! How art thou cut down to the ground, which didst weaken (subdued) the nations!* (13) *For thou hast said in thine heart, I will ascend (mount up) into heaven (heavens), I will exalt my throne above the stars of God; I will sit also upon the mount of the congregation, in the sides (recesses or secluded areas) of the north (the dwelling place of God).* (14) *I will ascend above the heights of the clouds (second heaven); I will be like the Most High.* (15) *Yet thou shalt be brought down to hell (the holding place of the ungodly), to the sides of the pit.*

So, the serpent, Lucifer, Satan, the devil, and the dragon, to mention some of his names, was more wise and crafty than any living being that the Lord (Yahweh) God had made; knowing evil and not ashamed to question the truth of God's words. He said unto the woman Eve: "Can it be that God really said," therefore, not really a question and not asking for information or for an answer, but to negate or invalidate, if you will, the word of God so as to bring doubt to what is positively truth. Thereby putting Eve in a mental state suspended between two or more propositions, infusing her mind with indecision causing uncertainty to the point of contradicting the word of God that she really knew to be true. He is the manipulator of the mind to distort the truth of the word of God, and opposition to God is Satan's sphere of activity. So he said to Eve, "Can it be that God has said you shall not eat from any tree in the garden?" Not that he didn't know the answer, but the devil wanted to know if Eve really understood the commands of God, testing her faculties.

Genesis 3:2—*And the woman said unto the serpent, We may eat of the fruit of the trees of the garden.* Then Eve said to the devil, "We [Adam and Eve] may eat from the fruit of trees," misquoting Genesis 2:16 by omitting the emphatic word "freely." Genesis 3:3—*But of the fruit of the tree which is in the midst of the garden, God hath said, you shall not eat of it, neither shall ye touch it, lest ye die.* So not only did Eve omit the word "freely" in verse 2, but here in verse 3, she again omits the emphatic word "surely," thus making it conditional and not emphatic, and she added words, "neither shall you touch it," which are not in Genesis 2:16–17, and neither did she specify which tree not to eat from, for there were two trees in the midst of the garden—the tree of life and the tree of knowledge of good and evil.

Knowing that the devil knows the mind of Eve, he proceeds to cast uncertainty and confusion upon her; incidentally, Adam was there all along while the devil was talking with Eve but did not interject. One thing to note is that God commanded the man Adam not to eat from the tree of knowledge of good and evil before Eve was formed. So it was up to the man Adam to pass over that command to Eve as the head. Now we don't know whether the man Adam passed over the command to Eve exactly as he received it from God for her to omit some words and add some other words at the same time. That's why I think first we have to be careful not to put all the blame on Eve because the man Adam was actually there when the devil was deceiving Eve. The word "touch," as added by Eve, has a connotation, among other things in Hebrew, of figuratively to lay with a woman and, by implication, to "reach or lay a hand upon," meaning a physical touch between two objects. I will say more on this subject as we go on so that we know exactly what the devil did.

Genesis 3:4–5—(4) *And the serpent said unto the woman, ye shall not surely die.* (5) *For God doth know that in the day ye eat thereof, then your eyes shall be opened, and ye shall be as gods, knowing good and evil.* The serpent, Satan, contradicted God's word, saying, "You shall not surely die," but God emphatically said, "You shall surely die." This is the foundation of the devil's plans and purpose to contradict and oppose the truth. John 8:44 says—*Ye are of your father the devil, and the lusts of your father ye will do. He was a murderer from the beginning, and abode not in the truth, because there is no truth in him. When he speaketh a lie, he speaketh of his own; for he is a liar, and the father of it.* The Lord Jesus Christ calls the devil, Satan, the father of liars. It is not that the devil does not know the word of God—that it is true—he just chose not to believe it because he is so full of himself; he wants to be like God. Christianity is the only religion that is literally based on the word of God. The devil is the father of all false religion, including all occults that base their religious worship on rites and ceremonies that are not Bible-based but are based on idols established by man. His second lie was to transfer the eminence of God to man and man having to make a choice about what he should believe and how he should live, and not of man believing in God and living according to God's commandments, thereby putting man to be the eminence of himself and not of God and, by doing so, making himself a god. This is the foundation of spiritism and the worship of demons and idols. The serpent lied to Eve and Adam, saying that by eating of the tree of knowledge of good and evil, their eyes would be opened to know good and evil, making them to be like God, because that was his plan from the beginning: to be like God. But to the contrary, their eyes were closed to only knowing God.

Genesis 3:6—*And when the woman saw that the tree was good for food, and that it was pleasant to the eyes, and a tree to be desired to make one wise, she took of the fruit thereof, and did eat, and gave also unto her husband with her; and he did eat.* When Eve perceived in her mind and visualized what was before her, the shining one, Satan, in all his beauty and perfection, with his cunningness, she was persuaded that indeed he was delightful for food and that he was pleasant to look at, which is the lust of the eyes. 1 John 2:16 says—*For all that is in the world, the lust of the flesh, and the lust of the eyes, and the pride of life, is not of the Father, but is of the world.* So she was deceived and persuaded that by eating the fruit of the tree, she would be wise. The devil himself has the source of wisdom. Let us equally divide the word of truth by comparing scripture with scripture so that we can establish this tree that was good for food and pleasant to the eyes, and a tree to make one wise.

Ezekiel 28:13–14 says—(13) *You were in Eden, the garden of God, every precious stone was your covering; the ruby, the topaz, and the diamond, the beryl, the onyx, and the jasper, the sapphire, the emerald, and the carbuncle, and gold; the workmanship of thy tabrets and of thy pipes was prepared in thee in the day that thou wast created, they were prepared.* (14) *Thou art the anointed cherub that covereth, and I have set thee so, thou wast upon the holy mountain of God; thou hast walked up and down in the midst of the stones of fire.* So now we see from scripture that the king of Tyre is the personification of the anointed cherub who is the supernatural being, the shining one, the devil, and Satan, and he is himself the tree that possesses knowledge of good and evil, the eminence of everything Eve. He was there in Eden, the garden of God; he is the serpent. The book of Genesis uses a lot of symbols, figures of speech, and numbers, just like the book of Revelation. Even though the serpent is the tree of knowledge of good and evil, he chooses not to do good because doing good is to glorify God, but he chooses to do evil so that he can glorify himself as a god.

Now that we have established that the serpent was actually there in the Garden of Eden and that the serpent is the anointed cherub—a powerful supernatural being who is Lucifer, the devil, Satan, and the dragon—let us establish what then rarely happened in the Garden of Eden. So after Eve was convinced, without a doubt, that by eating the fruit of the tree she would become wise and be as God—knowing good and evil—she took the fruit and ate it, and she also gave it to Adam, her husband, and he also ate the fruit. Now this expression is what is called a euphemism, meaning substitution of a word or expression that may be considered to be too offensive and vague with one that may seem mild or polite. For example, when you say, someone "passed away," that is a euphemism that describes the death of a person. So is the expression "She took of the fruit, thereof, and did eat and gave also unto her husband with her and he did eat it." This is a euphemism that literally means she had intercourse with the shining one, Satan himself, the devil; and yes—I know this may sound unthinkable and may come as a shock to some—Adam also participated in the act. For we are told that she gave also to her husband Adam and he ate.

Now, you may ask, how can this be a supernatural being and have intercourse with a woman and then the man? Well, for starters, Satan is a supernatural being and he can transform himself into whatever he wants to be, just like he transformed himself into an angel of light. 2 Corinthians 11:14—***And no marvel; for Satan himself in transformed into an angel of light.*** He can do whatever he desires to do to fulfill his wickedness to stop the will of God. We are also told of angels appearing in the scriptures as human beings. To prove that this truly occurred, that this super angel had intercourse with Eve, we go to scripture. Genesis 6:1–2 says—(1) ***And it came to pass, when men (the man Adam) began to multiply on the face of the earth, and daughters were born unto them (Adam and***

*Eve), (2) **That the sons of God saw the daughters of men that they were fair; and they took them wives of all which they chose.** And Genesis 6:4 says—**There were giants (Nephilim) in (upon) the earth in those days; and also after that, when the sons of God (angels) came in unto (had intercourse with) the daughters of men (the daughters of the man Adam), and they bare (bore) children to them, the same (giants) became mighty men which were of old, men of renown.** Then Jude 6 refers to these same angels saying—**And the angels which kept (preserved) not their first estate (principality), but left their own habitation (residence), he hath reserved in everlasting chains under darkness unto the judgement of the great day.** And 2 Peter 2:4 says—**For if God spared not the angels (fallen angels) that sinned, but cast them down to hell, (thrust down to Tartarus) and delivered them into chains of darkness to be reserved unto judgement.**

So we see if the angels left their abodes in the heaven's sphere and came to have intercourse with the daughters of Adam, why can't the devil himself, who is a supernatural angel, do the same? And the scripture proves that there were children born by these fallen angels called giants. A good example of these giants is Goliath, who was a descendant of the Nephilim, the one David killed in 1 Samuel 17:4—**And there went out a champion out of the camp of the Philistines, named Goliath, of Gath, whose height was six cubits and a span.** These were superhuman, abnormal beings, great in size as well as in wickedness, and they were also called, in Hebrew, *gibbor*, meaning "mighty men" or "the heroes that are renowned men"—renowned for their ungodliness. In Genesis 14:5 they're called Rephaims and Emins—**And in the fourteenth year came Chedorlaomer, and the kings that were with him, and smote the Rephaims in Ashteroth Karnaim, and the Zuzims in Ham, and the Emins in Shaveh Kiriathaim.** In Numbers 13:33 it says—**And there we saw the giants, the sons of Anak, which come of the giants; and we were in our own sight as grasshoppers, and so we were in their sight.**

This is why God brought the flood of Noah to destroy this hybrid, and the wickedness they brought upon the earth. After Noah's flood, there was another eruption of the fallen angels, and again children were born from this eruption. These fallen angels were part of the third of the angels who followed Lucifer, the devil, after he was cast down from the throne of God. In Matthew 25:41 it states—***Then shall he say also unto them on the left hand, Depart from me, ye cursed, into everlasting fire, prepared for the devil and his angels.*** The eruption of these fallen angels, which was before the flood of Noah, was to corrupt the bloodline of the woman of Genesis 3:15, from whom the promised seed (Jesus) of the woman would come. ***And I will put enmity between thee and the woman, and between thy seed and her seed; it shall bruise thy head, and thou shalt bruise his heel.*** The devil had a plan all along to make sure that the seed would not come by corrupting the bloodline of Adam.

The second eruption of the fallen angels was after the flood of Noah. The descendants of those children born settled in the promised land of Canaan before Abraham was called by God, who gave the promise of the land of milk and honey in which the Israelites would settle. So they occupied the Promised Land to prevent the Israelites from settling there. The devil's plan has always been to stop the will of God on the earth. He knew that the Messiah was to come through the bloodline of the man Adam and Eve, so he sent the fallen angels, referred to in Matthew 25:41, to corrupt the bloodline, knowing that God would not allow the Messiah to be born from a corrupt bloodline.

Now that we have established that the serpent is Satan, the devil, and that he had intercourse with Eve, we may now look at what came out of that adultery. It may shock many to know that the devil deposited his seed in the woman Eve, and Eve conceived of the devil, and that the seed was Cain, but Adam was the father of Abel, and Cain and Abel were twins. And yes, it is very much possible for a woman to have twins by two different men—highly unusual and rare but possible; you may ask your doctor. You may also ask, "How can you prove this?" Well, with scripture. 1 John 3:12 says—***Not as Cain, who was of that wicked one (evil one, the devil), and*** *slew his brother. And wherefore (for the sake of what) slew (slaughtered) he him? Because his own works were evil (full of labors and pains in working mischief), and his brother's righteous.* And John 8:44 says—*Ye are of your father the devil, and the lusts (desires) of your father ye will do. He was a murderer (manslayer) from the beginning (of the human race), and abode (stand firm) not in the truth, because there is no truth in him. When he speaketh a lie, he speaketh of his own (nature); for he is a liar, and the father of it.*

So we see that the devil is the father of many lies, and who is the first murderer? It was his son, Cain, who slayed his brother Abel without premeditation because of the desires of his father he was fulfilling. And the Lord Jesus Christ was telling the Pharisees that they were the sons of the devil, making them the descendants of Cain, because the desires (they were fulfilling) of their father, the devil, was to kill the Lord Jesus Christ. Now we know that Adam had intercourse with his wife, Eve, and thereby Eve conceived of the devil and Adam after God took them out of the Garden of Eden.

Genesis 3:7—*And the eyes of them both were opened, and they knew that they were naked. And they sewed fig leaves together, and made themselves aprons.* Their eyes were opened before they sinned but only to perceive good, but after they sinned, their eyes were opened to perceive good and also evil. It's not like they did not know before that they were naked, because Genesis 2:25 says—*And they were both naked, the man and his wife, and were not ashamed.* They were naked and not ashamed before they sinned, because their eyes were opened only to know good, but after they sinned, their perception received a new meaning, to know evil—that is, to know what is morally bad, the desires of the body and its consequences. Evil is the outward deed of a morally corrupt mind, and good is the inward deed of a morally just mind. Therefore, knowing good and evil puts a human being at battle within him- or herself. It's the battle between the good, God-given moral standards and the evil, everything that is morally bad. Our earthly bodies know only the things of this world. Knowing God leads to obedience, but knowing evil leads to disobedience; and disobedience leads to sin, and sin leads to death. Rebellion (disobedience) is as the sin of witchcraft. Since we have the knowledge of good and evil, we have the choice of what we obey, and what we obey, we live by; and what we live by, we become. Because Adam disobeyed God but obeyed the woman Eve, Adam lost the glorious likeness of God. This is what happens when we sin: we lose the glory of God because God hates evil. So when they came to know that they were naked, they made a covering for themselves out of the fig leaves to cover their shame. Sin brings shame to our body.

Genesis 3:8—***And they heard the voice (sound) of the Lord God walking (footsteps) in the garden in the cool (gentle breeze) of the day; and Adam and his wife hid themselves from the presence of the Lord God amongst the trees of the garden.*** It has always been the will of the Lord God to be with his children from the beginning of the heavens and the earth that are now. But when we sin, we hide ourselves in darkness from the presence of the Lord God, not knowing that when his brightness comes, it uncovers and exposes our nakedness because darkness can never overshadow his brightness. That's why we should live in the light, so that the glorious brightness of our Lord God should be our covering.

Genesis 3:9–10—(9) ***And the Lord (Yahweh) God called unto Adam (the man), and said unto him, Where art thou?*** (10) ***And he said, I heard thy voice in the garden, and I was afraid, because I was naked; and I hid myself.*** The first thing we should do when we sin is to run to God and not hide from Him, because only He can forgive our sins through His mercy, which is in Jesus Christ our savior, who is our covering. He is always seeking us, asking, "Where are you?"

CHAPTE 9:
THE BLAME GAME AND SHAME

Genesis 3:11–12—(11) ***And he said, Who told thee that thou wast naked? Hast thou eaten of the tree, whereof I commanded thee that thou shouldest not eat?*** (12) ***And the man (Adam) said, The woman whom thou gavest to be with me, she gave me of the tree, and I did eat.*** This is the nature of the human being, to blame others for causing us to sin when we know very well that we have the power and authority over anything the devil may put in front of us. Matthew 5:37 says—***But let your statement be, Yes, yes; No, no, and anything beyond these is from the evil one (the devil).*** Here we see the man Adam blaming the woman Eve for making him sin when he knew very well that Yahweh God commanded him not to eat from it. We should be bold enough to admit our wrongs, even when it brings shame to us. Psalms 51:17 says—***The sacrifices of God are a broken spirit; a broken and contrite heart, O God, thou wilt not despise.*** And Isaiah 57:15 says—***For thus saith the high and lofty One who resides forever, and whose name is Holy; I reside in a high and holy place, with*** *him also that is of a contrite and humble spirit, to revive the spirit of the humble, and to revive the heart of the contrite ones.* God delights in a humble and repentant heart that is filled with a sense of guilt and the desire to be forgiven. Genesis 3:13—*And the Lord (Yahweh) God said unto the woman, What is this that thou hast done? And the woman said, The serpent beguiled me, and I did eat.* We see also that the woman Eve blames the serpent. No one admitted to their wrong.

The Apostle Paul said the Corinthians used the same narrative as to what had happened to Eve in the Garden of Eden. 2 Corinthians 11:3 says—*But I fear, lest by means, as the serpent beguiled Eve through his subtilty, so your minds should be corrupted from the simplicity that is in Christ.* The word "beguiled," as used by the Apostle Paul, is the same word used by Eve, and it means "to seduce wholly"; it's a stronger word than "deceive," in Greek (*"exapatao"*) and carries the same connotation in Hebrew (*"nasha"*), which means to be led astray in your mind and judgment.

Brothers and sisters in Christ the Lord, if you believe the word of God to be true, then you have to understand and know what truly happened in the Garden of Eden. Eve was wholly seduced; therefore, her mind and judgment were captured by the beauty and cunning of the serpent, Satan, the devil, and by that she was led astray and had sexual intercourse with the devil, a supernatural being. If you are a Christian and believe that Eve ate an apple—by the way, every tree in the garden was given to them by Yahweh God to eat freely from, including "the" apple tree—you have believed a lie from the father of liars, the devil. This is how Eve conceived the seed of the evil one, and that seed was Cain.

This is one of the things that compelled me to write this book that, by the grace of God, was given to me to bring the truth to light. After my conversion six years ago, one of the things I asked God was for Him to teach me His word, and He gave me the answer, to know His word. I started to study His word, spending hours and hours at the library and at home. I gave my life wholly to Him by surrendering all that I was, full of sin, to Him. I repented of every sin I could remember, and I forgave all who had done wrong to me and who I had wronged. After much crying and much prayer, and much questioning of God about why things had not worked out in my life, I felt the weight of sorrow and disappointment lifted away from me, and by that I knew God had forgiven me, and He sent His spirit to abide in me and on me, and He told me at night to "permeate." I did not know the meaning of the word "permeate," but I woke up during the night and I wrote it down; in the morning, I looked it up in the dictionary, and it simply said, "To pass through." So God was telling me to go through everything that was coming in my life. Yes, for you to be called a son of God, God will allow the devil to come at you in full force just like He did to Job and the Lord Jesus Christ, who had to go through suffering, humiliation, and the death of an evildoer for us all to receive forgiveness and salvation. One of the things Yahweh God gave me was the grace to know His word, which I have loved; it's now my life to know the truth and to tell the truth that is in His word. It takes the love of His word to know God. It doesn't come easily; it's a life commitment.

Genesis 3:14—*And the Lord (Yahweh) God said unto the serpent, Because thou hast done this, thou art cursed above all cattle, and above every beast of the field; upon thy belly shalt thou go, and dust shalt thou eat all the days of thy life.* If you take notice, Yahweh God did not ask the serpent, the devil, any questions, but he proceeded to pass judgment upon him, saying, "You will be cursed more than any domesticated animal and more than any wild animal. ""On your belly you shall go," is a figure of speech implying the utmost humiliation and degradation, and "dust shalt thou eat" implies the state of utter defeat.

Genesis 3:15—*And I will put enmity (hostility) between thee and the woman (Eve), and between thy seed (through Cain) and her seed (Jesus Christ); it (he, Jesus Christ) shall bruise (strike) thy head, and thou shalt bruise (strike) his heel.* Yahweh God continues with the judgment, saying to Satan that He will put hostility—that is, aggressive behavior—between Satan and Eve, and between the offspring of Satan through Cain, and the offspring of Eve through Seth. The offspring of Eve through Isaac is Jesus Christ, which is singular in Hebrew text. He is the same seed implied in Genesis 21:12, which says—*And God said unto Abraham, Let it not be grievous in thy sight because of the lad (Ishmael), and because of thy bondwoman (Hagar); in all that Sarah hath said unto thee, hearken unto her voice; for in Isaac shall thy seed (singular, meaning Jesus Christ) be called.* And he's also the seed referred to in Galatians 3:16, which says— *Now to Abraham and his seed (singular, Christ Jesus) were the promises made (spoken). He saith not, And to seeds (plural), as of many; but as of one (Christ Jesus), And to thy seed, which is Christ.*

Christ Jesus, being the seed of the woman Eve, shall strike the devil's head (figure of speech as to a vital part of the body of a person), implying the utter destruction of Satan and his works on the earth after the one-thousand-year rule of the King of kings and the Lord of lords, when he will be utterly defeated and completely destroyed in the lake of fire (this is still in the future), but he won't go without a fight. He struck the seed of the woman, the Christ at Calvary, which was temporal, on his heel, which is the lower part of the body. If someone strikes you on the head, you can die, but if someone strikes you on your feet, you suffer pain.

Hebrews 2:14 says—*Forasmuch then as the children are partakers (sharers) of flesh and blood, he also himself likewise (in like manner) took part (shared) of the same (same things); that (in order) through death he might (could) destroy him (the devil) that had (holding) the power (strength) of death, that is, the devil.* And 1 John 3:8 says—*He that committeth sin is of the devil; for the devil sinneth from the beginning (of humanity). For this purpose the Son of God (Jesus Christ) was manifested (visible), that he (Jesus Christ) might destroy (to demolish or tear down) the works of the devil.* This is the first great prophecy and promise concerning the coming Messiah and the destruction of the devil. The coming of the seed Messiah has already been fulfilled, but the destruction of the devil is still in the future.

CHAPTER 10:
SUBJECT, RULE, SUBMIT (NOT NECESSARILY IN THAT ORDER)

Genesis 3:16—*Unto the woman he said, I will greatly multiply thy sorrow and thy conception; in sorrow thou shalt bring forth children (sons); and thy desire shall be to thy husband and he shall rule over thee.* And to Eve, Yahweh God said, "I will greatly multiply"; that is, "I will multiply Hebrewism," emphasizing the double distress coming before her that is the double conception of the sons, Cain by the devil and Abel by Adam, because they were twins. Therefore, when a woman is pregnant with twins, she goes through more distress and pain at birth than a woman who is pregnant with one child. And Yahweh God continues by saying, "And their desire shall be to thy husband," which means to subject your husband to whatever shall be your desire. Yahweh God knew that because Adam listened to his wife Eve to also eat from the tree of knowledge of good and evil, she will subject her husband to do whatever she desires for the man Adam to do, hence the punishment of Adam in Genesis 3:17

which says—*And unto Adam he said, Because thou hast hearkened unto the voice of thy wife, and hast eaten of the tree, of which I commanded thee, saying, Thou shalt not eat of it: cursed is the ground for thy sake; in sorrow shalt thou eat of it all the days of thy life.*

But Yahweh God, knowing this, still instituted the man Adam to rule over the woman Eve as the head of the house. Satan knew that the woman was a weaker vessel, and that is why he went to the woman first, and through the woman Eve, he got the man Adam. It worked then, and he is still doing it; the devil's ways never change. It was true then and it is true now that wives subject their husbands to their desires, and I am not saying that it's all totally bad for a wife to subject her husband. It's bad only when her desires are selfish and not pleasing to God. The devil knows that men have a soft spot for women, and he uses that as a weapon to bring men down. But when a wife subjects her husband to the things that are in accordance with and pleasing to God, that husband is blessed. Proverbs 31:10–12 says—(10) *A woman of excellence, who will find? For her worth is far more than precious jewels.* (11) *The heart of her husband trusts in her, and gain he will not lack.* (12) *She does him good and not harm all the days of her life.* And verse 20 says—*She opens her arms to the poor and reaches out her hands to the needy.* And verse 30 says— *Charm is deceptive, and beauty is fleeting, but a woman who fears the Lord is to be praised.* And Yahweh God continues to say to the woman, "Even though your desires will be to subject your husband, he shall still rule over you." The Apostle Paul said in Colossians 3:18—*Wives submit yourselves to your husbands, as is fitting in the Lord.* And the Apostle Peter said in 1 Peter 3:1—*Wives, in the same way, submit yourselves to your own husbands so that, even if some are disobedient to the word, they may be won over without a word, by the conduct of their wives.* There is just something about the word "submit" that ticks women off in a wrong way; go figure.

CHAPTER 11:
SEED

Now, the word "seed" has two symbolic meanings in the word of God. In Hebrew the seed, as implied here by Yahweh God, means "posterity" or "progeny," and in Greek it means "sperma." This is why Yahweh God said to the serpent, "I will put hostility between your seed," which is the devil's progeny and woman's seed, which is Eve's posterity. Because Yahweh God knew what the serpent, Satan, did to Eve in the Garden of Eden, which was that the serpent deposited his sperma in Eve and the progeny was Cain, and the seed of the woman implied here is Jesus Christ, who is the posterity of Eve. Galatians 3:16—*Now to Abraham and his seed were the promises made. He saith not, And to seeds, as of many; but as of one, And to thy seed, which is Christ.* And Genesis 21:12—*And God said unto Abraham, Let it not be grievous in thy sight because of the lad, and because of thy bondwoman; in all that Sarah hath said unto thee, hearken unto her voice; for in Isaac shall thy seed be called.* The other meaning of "seed" in the word of God is figuratively, the word of God. Luke 8:11 says—*Now the parable is this (means or represents): The seed is the word of God.*

Genesis 3:17—*And unto Adam he said, Because thou hast hearkened unto the voice of thy wife, and hast eaten of the tree, of which I commanded thee, saying, Thou shalt not eat of it: cursed is the ground for thy sake; in sorrow shalt eat of it all the days of thy life.* This is one of the points I was narrating in the previous account. Adam was not supposed to take orders from Eve; therefore, by doing so, he failed as the head of his house and as the head of his domain. As a result of that, he forfeited his authority to his wife and at the same time, because he ate of the tree of knowledge of good and evil, he forfeited his authority and control of his domain to the devil. That's why the devil would say to the Lord Jesus Christ when he was being tempted in the wilderness in Luke 4:6—*And the devil said unto him, All this power will I give thee, and the glory of them: for that is delivered unto me; and to whomsoever I will I give it.*

The man Adam handed over the domain that Yahweh God had put under him to rule. And just as he lost his authority to his wife as the head of his house by listening to her, Yahweh God still instituted him as the head over his wife and thus created the battle of the sexes—the husband having the tendency of dominant control over his wife and the wife having the tendency of dominance over her husband. Because of Adam's sin, Yahweh God cursed the ground instead of putting a curse on Adam. Adam was now to till the ground for his food because Yahweh God removed him from the Garden of Eden, where the provision of food was free. Genesis 3:18–19— (18) *Thorns also and thistles shall it bring forth to thee; and thou shalt eat the herb of the field;* (19) *In the sweat of thy face shalt thou eat bread (bread), till thou return unto the ground; for out of it wast thou taken: for dust thou art and unto dust shalt thou return.* This judgment takes away the provision of "freely you may eat" and puts it on the man Adam to fend for himself and his family. In toil he shall eat the food through all kinds of elements and difficulties. He was to till the ground and eat from the green vegetation of the field instead of the fruits from the trees in the garden. This was the beginning of agriculture and keeping of domesticated animals with difficulty and stress. The word "bread" means all kinds of food. This judgment also came with the sentence of death, as Yahweh God had said to Adam, "You shall surely die."

CHAPTER 12:
MIND, BODY, SPIRIT

Genesis 3:20–21—(20) ***And Adam called his wife's name Eve (life spring); because she was the mother of all living (all who should live after her). (21)—Unto Adam also and to his wife did the Lord God make coats of skins, and clothed them.*** "Eve" means "life" in Hebrew; therefore, she is the life springer of all who should live after her. But this only applies to one race, the Israelites. She is the life springer or mother of all the Israelites, and this shows that Adam believed God by faith that she will bring forth children, hence the name Eve. The seed of the woman that would bruise the head of the serpent was to come only through this race that would spring from Eve, who would not only bruise the head of the serpent but would come as the Messiah to release humankind from the bondage of sin in this world. The grace and mercy of Yahweh God is here portrayed by Him sacrificing an animal to cover the shame of Adam and Eve. Just as He came in a sinful nature to be our sacrifice for our shame and the sins of this world age and his blood being our covering, His mercy and grace is beyond our comprehension and endures from generation to generation.

Genesis 3:22–24—(22) *And the Lord God said, Behold, the man (Adam) is become as one of us, to know good (general good) and evil: and now, lest he put forth his hand, and take also of the tree of life, and eat, and live forever:* (23) *Therefore the Lord God sent him forth from the Garden of Eden, to till the ground from whence he was taken.* (24) *So, he drove out the man; and he placed (to dwell) at the east of the Garden of Eden, cherubim (plural) and a flaming sword which turned every way, to keep the way of the tree of life.* Yahweh God, knowing that the man Adam had now become conscious not only of knowing moral good but of evil desires, had to take the man Adam and his wife out of the garden before he could put his hands on the fruit of the tree of life and live forever in a sinful nature. This would have been unthinkable and unspeakable for Yahweh God, knowing the nature of the man Adam's ability, now to desire evil and to be easily seduced, and enticed, by what is desirable to the eyes and body of all that is earthly. Yahweh God could not take a chance for the man to remain in the garden with the tree of life. You see, our natural desires are what we are told not to do. Our natural mind and body gravitate only to what is earthly and not to what is heavenly, because we're not able to discern things of the spirit. So it's up to us as born-again Christians, in our inner self, through whom we receive the things of the spirit, to put under subjection our natural mind and body to the things of the spirit. It's up to us to control our minds and the desires of the body. When you are able to control your mind and body, you are complete in Christ and have become a mature Christian. Yahweh God, knowing this, sent the man Adam out of the garden, and then Yahweh God put cherubim on the east of the Garden of Eden with a flaming sword that turned every way to preserve the way to the tree of life. Remember, cherubim are celestial spirit beings; they are angels of the highest order, just as Lucifer, the serpent, is the devil. Ezekiel 28:14—*Thou art the anointed cherub (singular) that covereth; and I have set thee so: thou wast upon the holy mountain of God; thou hast walked up and down in the midst of the stones of fire.*

CHAPTER 13:
IF GOD SAID IT, THEN IT'S THE TRUTH

Genesis 4:1–2—(1)—*And Adam knew Eve his wife; and she conceived (became pregnant), and bare Cain, and said, I have gotten a man from the Lord. (2) And she again bare his brother Abel. And Abel was a keeper of sheep, but Cain was a tiller of the ground.* After Adam and Eve were taken out of the garden, Adam knew his wife. The word "knew" is a euphemism, substituting as a mild word for one thought to be offensive. So the correct rendering should be Adam had sexual intercourse with his wife, Eve, and she became pregnant. When the time came for her to give birth, she gave birth to Cain first and continued to give birth to Abel. The word "again," as rendered here in Hebrew, means "once more," thereby making Cain and Abel twins—Cain the son of the devil and Abel the son of Adam. Now the use of euphemisms has changed the word of God in some ways. I don't know why the translators could not just say what the word of God said, so that people will know the truth. If God said it, then it's the truth. We should rather be more emphatic and straight to the point when it comes to the word of God, so that people will not be misled by or misunderstand what God intended to portray. This is why I caution the use of the new translation Bibles, because some have veered away from the original Hebrew and Greek texts and, by so doing, have changed the meaning of some words altogether. The devil has taken advantage of this to subvert the truth, and, if I might add, it's more deliberate now than ever, and this has led Christians to be tepid.

The name Cain means "acquisition" and Abel means "transitory"; hence, his life was cut short. As they grew older, Cain became a farmer and Abel became a shepherd. I believe this was by revelation from Yahweh God. Nothing just happens without God's foreknowledge.

Genesis 4:3–5—(3) *And in the process of time (at the end of days) it came to pass that Cain brought of the fruit of the ground an offering unto the Lord (Yahweh).* (4) *And Abel, he also brought of the firstlings (choicest) of his flock and of the fat thereof. And the Lord (Yahweh) had respect (looked with favor) unto Abel and to his offering:* (5) *But unto Cain and to his offering he had not respect. And Cain was very wroth (angry), and his countenance fell (his face fell).* So in the process of time. Therefore, at the end of days or time, probably an appointed place was made for them by Yahweh God. This was again by revelation or a command of Yahweh God because, as I said, nothing just happens with God, and both Cain and Abel knew of the time and place, and what to bring for an offering. The only thing they were not told was the choice of what to bring to offer Yahweh. Yahweh God was testing their faith and their reverence, so they both brought by faith. Faith is living by the divinely implanted principal that comes by hearing, and hearing the word implanted, and not just hearing but acting upon the word collectively. Romans 10:17 says—*Consequently, faith comes by hearing, and hearing through the word of Christ.* So they both received this divine principle, but the difference was in their reverence of who Yahweh was in their lives, and this is also true even in our own lives to this day. Psalm 111:10 says— *The fear (reverence) of the Lord is the beginning of wisdom: a good understanding have all they that do his commandments (precepts); his praise endureth forever.* And Proverbs 9:10 says—*The fear of the Lord (Yahweh) is the beginning (start and not the end) of wisdom (the ability to make the right choice); and the knowledge of the holy (holy ones of majesty) is the understanding (discernment).* Proverbs 1:7 states—*The fear of the Lord (Yahweh) is the beginning of knowledge, but fools despise wisdom and instruction.* So when the time came as instructed and appointed by Yahweh, Cain brought from the harvest of the ground, which God had cursed, but Cain had no fear of Yahweh to offer the firstlings and the fattest of his grain in recognition of his sovereignty over nature. And because of his lack of fear toward God, he showed no reverence for Yahweh and the occasion, just like his father, the devil, who has no fear of God. But because of the fear of God Abel had, by faith he brought the firstlings and the fattest ones too, and Yahweh had favorable regards for Abel (but not for Cain) and accepted it by consuming it by fire.

Genesis 4:6–7—(6) *And the Lord said unto Cain, Why art thou wroth? And why is thy countenance fallen?* (7) *If thou doest well, shalt thou not be accepted? And if thou doest not well, sin lieth at the door. And unto thee shall be (is) his (its) desire, and thou shalt rule over him (it).* Cain was angry that Yahweh did not accept his offering, and his face fell. He was not angry with God for not accepting his offering, but he was angry with Abel for doing well. Anger builds up hate, and hate leads to evil desires. He became jealous of his brother Abel, but Yahweh, full of mercy and grace, said to Cain, "If you do well—that is, if you follow my instruction and honor me with the firstlings of your fruits—I will accept your offering, but if you don't follow my instruction and honor me, at the entrance lies a sin offering. That is to accept your wrongs by bringing a sin offering, and by doing so, you will rule over the desires to sin. It is the same expression used in Genesis 3:16 when Yahweh God says to the woman Eve, "Your desire is to subject your husband under you, but even with that desire, your husband will still rule over you."

So even with Yahweh telling Cain what to do, he was burning with indignation toward Yahweh for not accepting his offering and the spirit of jealously came into him over his brother Abel. Jealousy leads to all sorts of evil intents, and evil intents, if not brought under subjection, will give in to evil acts. You see that in Cain, who had all the attributes of his father, the devil. His mind was not set on pleasing Yahweh God but on exhuming the desires of his father, Satan, the shining one. Cain is the fullness and express image (body) of his father, the devil. If we follow the commandments of Yahweh God and do them, we will know without a doubt the right offering to Yahweh. It's by faith that we please God, and by doing so, Yahweh will accept our offerings. Genesis 4:8—*And Cain talked with Abel his brother; and it came to pass, when they were in the field, that Cain rose up against Abel his brother, and slew him.* This verse should be rightly rendered as follows, according to the original Hebrew text: "Then Cain said to his brother Abel, let us go into the field, and when they were in the field, Cain rose up against his brother Abel and killed him."

Now we see the exhumed indignation, jealousy, and hate come out into action. This is what happens when any sort of deep indignation is allowed to grow in our hearts. It explodes into action that cannot be reversed. Religion has been from the beginning of humanity the greatest cause of bloodshed in the world. The first death was due to worship; Abel's religion was found righteous to Yahweh God, but Cain's was found unrighteous. This was the beginning of worshipping. There is only one form of true religion, and that is the worship of the one true God, the Creator. Any religion that worships other gods, whether man or manmade, or worships any created thing, such as the sun, the moon, and the stars, or that worships demons, are all false religions and are all under the rule of the devil. So Cain, the son of the devil, was the first murderer. 1 John 3:12 proves that Cain was the son of the devil, and it says—*Not as Cain, who was of that wicked one, and slew his brother.* And for what reason did he violently murder him? Because his deeds were evil and the deeds of his brother were righteous. John 8:44 says—*You are of your father, the devil, and you want to do the desires of your father. He was a murderer from the beginning, and does not stand in the truth because there is no truth in him. Whenever he speaks a lie, he speaks from his own nature, for he is a liar and the father of lies.* So the Lord Jesus Christ put the Pharisees to be the sons of the devil, making them to be the descendants of Cain, because in them, just as it was in Cain, was the desire of their father, the devil. The Pharisees were filled with jealousy and hate, and were plotting to kill the Lord Jesus Christ.

Genesis 4:9–15—(9) *And the Lord (Yahweh) said unto Cain, Where is Abel thy brother? And he said, I know not; Am I my brother's keeper?* (10) *And he (the Lord) said, What hast thou done? The voice of thy brother's blood crieth unto me from the ground.* (11) *And now art thou cursed from the earth, which hath opened her mouth to receive thy brother's blood from thy hand;* (12) *When thou tillest the ground, it shall not henceforth yield unto thee her strength; a fugitive and vagabond shalt thou be in the earth (ground).* (13) *And Cain said unto the Lord, My punishment is greater than I can bear.* (14) *Behold, thou hast driven me out this day from the face of the earth; and from thy face shall I be hid; and I shall be a fugitive and a vagabond in the earth; and it shall come to pass, that every one that findeth me shall slay me.* (15) *And the Lord said unto him: Therefore, whosoever slayeth Cain, vengeance shall be taken on him sevenfold. And the Lord set a mark upon Cain, lest any finding him should kill him.* Yahweh asked Cain where his brother was, and like father, like son—full of lies—he lied about not knowing where his brother was. But Yahweh, the all-knowing God, knew already what he had done and cursed him more than the ground He had cursed in Genesis 3:17 for the sake of Adam. And Yahweh said to Cain, "When you till the ground that is cursed, it shall not give you a good harvest, and it will make you wander about looking for food and land, and always will be transitory." Then Cain asked Yahweh, "Is my iniquity too great to be forgiven?" Iniquity is a course of bad conduct flowing from the evil desire of a fallen nature and not the breaching or breaking of the law. So Yahweh sent him away from his presence.

You see, the presence of Yahweh is our covering from the elements that may come against us. Cain was afraid of retribution from anyone who would find him and know about what he had done to his brother, that they would be scared of him (Cain) and would instead kill him. But Yahweh said to him, "Not so," and he put a sign that characteristically would prevent anyone from killing him. So Cain left the presence of Yahweh, which was a place appointed by Yahweh for worship and offering. Now, you may ask, "Who are those ("everyone") referred to by Cain in verse 14?" Well, we are not told that Adam and Eve had other children at this point in time other than Cain and Abel, and after Cain murdered Abel, Cain was the only child they had, so then who is this "everyone" and/ or "whoever" that is referred to? We forget that God made other races in Genesis 1:26 before he formed Adam and Eve. So there was another race living outside the perimeter of the Garden of Eden, and this was the land that Yahweh God had permitted Adam and Eve to dwell in after they were taken out of the Garden of Eden.

Genesis 4:16–17—(16) *And Cain went out from the presence of the Lord (Yahweh), and dwelt in the land of Nod, on the east of Eden.* (17) *And Cain knew (had sexual intercourse) his wife; and she conceived, and bare Enoch: and he builded a city, and called the name of the city, after the name of his son, Enoch.* After Cain left the presence of Yahweh in the land appointed by Yahweh for worship, he went and settled in the land east of the Garden of Eden called Nod. "Nod" means "wandering"; hence, the land of nomads. And this is where "everyone" he mentioned in verse 14, who he was afraid would kill him dwelt (resided), and this is where he found his wife. I know that some preachers have said that Adam and Eve had other children before Cain killed Abel, and Cain might have taken one of his sisters and married her, but there is no proof of that, and we are told that Adam and Eve had other children after the birth of Seth in Genesis 5:3–4—(3) *And Adam lived an hundred and thirty years, and begat a son in his own likeness, and after his image; and called his name Seth.* (4) *And the days of Adam after he had begotten Seth were eight hundred years; and he begat sons and daughters.*

Genesis 4:25–26—(25) *And Adam knew his wife again; and she bare a son, and called his name Seth; for God, said she, hath appointed me another seed (son) instead of Abel, whom Cain slew. (26) And to Seth, to him also there was born a son, and he called his name Enos; then began men to call upon the name of the Lord.* And Adam had sexual intercourse with his wife again. The word "again" here means "following"; therefore after the death of Abel, she conceived and bore a son, Seth. "Seth" means "appointed" or "substituted." It was through Seth that the seed of woman was to come. God appointed Seth to be born as a substitute for Abel. There is just no indication that Adam and Eve had other children before the death of Abel but that Seth was the first child after the death of Abel, but they did have sons and daughters after Seth: Genesis 5:4–5—(4) *And the days of Adam after he had begotten Seth were eight hundred years; and he begat sons and daughters. (5) And all the days that Adam lived were nine hundred and thirty years; and he died.*

Seth also bore a son and called his name Enos, which means "frail" or "incurable." Then it was at this period of time, after the birth of Enos, that men began to call upon the name of Yahweh. This does not mean that they began to worship Yahweh. To the contrary, they began to profane the name of Yahweh by calling their idols Yahweh because the worship of Yahweh began with Abel, who offered a righteous offering to Yahweh, and Yahweh had favorable regards toward Abel. Enos is included with these people who started profaning the name of Yahweh, though he was the son of Seth, because he was part of this generation who went the way of Cain. This makes sense because if this generation surely worshipped Yahweh in truth, then what was Enoch, the seventh from Adam, prophesying against? It was because this was the beginning of lawlessness and idol worship, and Enoch, knowing through revelation from Yahweh of the lawlessness and unrighteousness that was going on in that generation, prophesied by faith. Jude 14 and 15 says—(14) *And Enoch, the seventh from Adam, prophesied about these people, saying; Behold the Lord came with ten thousands of his holy ones, (15) to execute judgement against all and to convince all that are ungodly among them of all their ungodly among them of all their ungodly deeds which they have ungodly committed, and all their hard speeches which ungodly sinners have spoken against him.*

Not only on the ungodly but also on the fallen angels who came and took the daughters of the man Adam and bore children to them. These children were hybrids and abnormal in size and in wickedness. So because of the increase in ungodly deeds, God had to bring the flood of Noah to destroy this generation that profaned his name and the progeny of the fallen angels, and to preserve Adam's race from whom the seed of the woman (Eve) was to come that would continue through Noah's family. Hebrews 10:31—***It is a terrifying thing to fall into the hands of the living God.***

CHAPTER 14:
THE FAMILY HISTORY OF THE MAN ADAM

Genesis 5:1–2—(1) ***This is the book of generations of Adam. In the day that God created man (the man Adam), in the likeness of God (Elohim) made he (God) him (Adam); (2) Male and female created he (God) them (Adam and Eve); and blessed them, and called their name Adam (mankind), in the day when they were created.*** Verses 1 and 2 should be rightly rendered as follows: This is the record of the generations of the man Adam when God (Elohim the Creator) created the man, Adam. He (God) made him (the man Adam) in the likeness of God; male and female, he (God) created them (Adam and Eve), and blessed them (Adam and Eve). And he called their name mankind or humankind when they were created. By this we have to understand and know emphatically that the emphasis is about the man Adam and Eve, his wife. And also, by this we have to know that God created all humankind, which are all races in his image. Therefore, a formed figure as a symbol (or model) of him on the earth, but only the man Adam was created in the likeness of God as a representative of God. We as humankind were to function in likeness of God morally, and that's why we are all born sinners, because we are all born with the sin of the man Adam, which is called the original sin. Through this same man Adam, God was to present his divine nature and divine will to his creation, but because of the fall of the man Adam, God could not present himself divinely to his creation. That's why he had to send his only begotten son, the second Adam, our Lord Jesus Christ, so that through Him He may establish His divine nature and divine will to His creation. But for Him to achieve that, He first had to redeem humanity and His creation from the original sin of the first man Adam that led to death. And the only way that was to be done was for the second Adam to be a sacrifice, and as we know, the Lord Jesus Christ went through suffering and was crucified and died, and after three days He rose again. His blood became our covering both for the original sin and our personal sins we committed before we came to Jesus Christ and were born again. The sins we commit after we have received Christ Jesus and are born again have been paid in full, but we have to ask God the Father for forgiveness in Christ Jesus's name.

There are fourteen generations in the Bible, of which eleven are in the book of Genesis. One is in the book of Numbers 3:1, which is the generation of Aaron and Moses; one is in the book of Ruth 4:18–22, which is the generation of Pharez; and the last one is in the book of Matthew 1:1, which is the generation of the Lord Jesus, and that makes up the fourteen generations. The number fourteen is a multiple of seven, which is the number of spiritual completeness or perfection. But of the fourteen generations, only two are actual titled genealogy of pedigree, which are the genealogy of the first man Adam in the book of Genesis 5 and the genealogy of the second man Adam (Jesus Christ) in the book of Matthew 1:1–16. The other twelve are titled family history or records.

Therefore, verses 1 and 2 give us the history of the creation of the man Adam and his wife, Eve. The first Adam was created in the likeness of God to be a representative of God's divine nature, but he failed the test because of the devil. In the same way, the second Adam came in the form of the first Adam, but without sin, and was also tested by the devil in the wilderness and overcame the deception and lies of the devil, and now we see the divine nature and divine will of God in him and through him. And just as we were born sinners by nature, by the sin of the first Adam, we are now overcomers through Jesus Christ, by His triumph over the devil.

Romans 5:12 says—***Wherefore, as by one man (Adam) sin entered into the world, and death by sin; and so death passed upon all men, for that all have sinned.*** So we see that sin entered into the world, which is now in 2 Peter 3:7, through the first man, Adam, and that sin led to death, so because the first Adam failed the test because of the devil, we are all sinners and we are all liable to die. Romans 5:13–19 says—(13) ***For until the law sin was in the world (which is now) but sin is not charged to one's account when there is no law.*** (14) ***Nevertheless death reigned from Adam to Moses, even over them that had not sinned after the similitude of Adam's transgression, who is the figure of him that was to come (the Lord Jesus Christ).*** (15) ***But not as the offence, so also is the free gift. For if through the offence (a falling aside when one should have stood upright) of one man (first Adam) many be dead, much more the grace of God, and the gift by grace, which is by one man, Jesus Christ, hath abounded unto many.*** (16) ***And not as it was by one that sinned, so is the gift; for the judgement was by one to condemnation, but the free gift is of many offences unto justification.*** (17) ***For if by one man's (Adam's) offence death reigned by one; much more they which receive abundance of grace and of the gift of righteousness shall reign in life by one, Jesus Christ.*** (18) ***Therefore, as by the offence of one judgement came upon all men to condemnation; even so by the righteousness of one the free gift came upon all men unto justification of life.*** (19) ***For as by one man's (the first Adam) disobedience many were made sinners, so by the obedience of one (Jesus Christ) shall many be made righteous.***

The first man Adam was a figure (image) of the Messiah Jesus Christ. The second Adam was who gave himself in the form of the first Adam as a sinner, though without sin, to be a sacrifice for all humanity that we might be justified and receive the free gift of righteousness from God the Father, by one righteous deed, the death on the cross. We are justified and made righteous from the sin of the first Adam and our own sins we might have committed before accepting Jesus Christ as our only Savior and Lord. We give God the Father all the honor and all the glory for His abundance of love, mercy, and grace for us all. And to our Lord Jesus Christ for being our Passover sacrifice, for by His blood we are justified and made righteous. By his death and resurrection, we have overcome the judgment of death, to the praise and glory of His holy name, because only He is wealthy, holy, faithful, righteous, and mighty, hallelujah!

Genesis 5:3—*And Adam lived an hundred and thirty years, and begat a son in his own likeness, and after his image; and called his name Seth.* Now this establishes the age of Adam from his creation to the birth of Seth, 130 years. We are not told how old Adam was when Cain and Abel were born, but I think the birth of Seth came slightly after the death of Abel. Hence, the meaning of Seth, "appointed" or "substituted" for Abel, and therefore God would continue his will through the lineage of Seth of whom the seed of the woman (Eve) was to come. This is a specific race chosen by God. After the birth of Seth, Adam had sons and daughters and died at the age of 930, for God said to Adam, "Surely you shall die."

Seth fathered Enos, meaning "frail or incurable." Enos fathered Cainan, meaning "a possession." Cainan fathered Mahalaleel, meaning "praise of God." Mahalaleel fathered Jared, meaning "descent." Jared fathered Enoch, meaning "teaching or initiation." Enoch was the seventh from Adam. The number seven means spiritual perfection. Enoch walked with God, meaning to and fro; that is, he lived a righteous life that gratified God entirely. And because of his righteous life, God took him. Hebrews 11:5 says—*By faith Enoch was translated that he should not experience death; and was not found because God translated him up, that before his removal, he had been approved as having been pleasing to God.* The word "translated" means to transport to a different place. So he was transported from the earth realm to heaven's realm. Now we know that flesh and blood cannot inherit heaven, so his body was transformed (metamorphosed); therefore, his body was changed in appearance and form. By faith, Enoch prophesied divinely instructed by God.

Jude 1:14–15 says—(14) *And Enoch also, the seventh from Adam, prophesied of these, saying, Behold, the Lord cometh with ten thousand of his saints,* (15) *To execute judgement upon all, and to convince all that are ungodly among them of their ungodly deeds which they have ungodly committed, and of all their hard speeches which ungodly sinners have spoken against him.* So Enoch was translated just as Elijah was in 2 Kings 2:9 without seeing death. *And it came to pass, when they were gone over, that Elijah said unto Elisha, Ask what I shall do for thee, before I be taken away from thee. And Elisha said, I pray thee, let a double portion of thy spirit be upon me.* A lot of wickedness was happening in that generation, all the way to Noah, and it all started with Cain; lawlessness and Enos's idol-worshipping, and then the influx of the fallen angels as in 2 Peter 2:4 that had sexual intercourse with the daughters of Adam, and giants, called the Nephilim, were born from them. God had to destroy this generation and, hence, the flood of Noah. Only two people we know of in the Bible were translated by God: Enoch and the prophet Elijah. But we know that those who are alive and righteous in Christ at the time of the Lord's coming shall be translated in a like manner.

1 Corinthians 15:50–53 says—(50) *But I say this, brothers, the flesh and blood is not able to inherit the kingdom of God, nor can corruption (liable to die mortal) inherit incorruptibility (immortal—not liable to die).* (51) *Behold, I tell you a mystery (secret) we will not all fall asleep (die) but we will all be changed (made different).* (52) *In a moment (indivisible unit [Atom] of time), in the twinkling (instant blink) of an eye, at the last trump; for the trumpet shall sound, and the dead shall be raised imperishable (incorruptible) and we (who are living) will be changed (made different).* (53) *For it is necessary for this perishable body to put on incorruptibility (immortal—not liable to die) and this mortal body (liable to die) to put on immortality (deathlessness).*

And 1 Thessalonians 4:13–18 says—(13) *But I do not want you to be ignorant, brothers, concerning those who have fallen asleep (died) so that you will not grieve as also the rest who have no hope.* (14) *For if we believe that Jesus died and rose again, even so them also which sleep (have died) in Jesus will God bring with him.* (15) *For this we say unto you by the word of the Lord, that we who are alive and remain (survive) until the Lord's coming, will not possibly precede (stand in the way of) those who have fallen asleep.* (16) *For the Lord himself will descend from heaven with a shout of command, the voice of the archangel (Michael) and with a trumpet of God, and the dead in Christ will rise first (boldly);* (17) *Then we who are alive and remain (survive), will be snatched,* as in being raptured—the word "rapture" is a Latin word meaning "caught up" and in Greek, as it is written, means "snatched up "(at the same place at once) *with them in the clouds (and a multitude of angels, therefore a throng of heavenly beings), to meet (encounter) the Lord in the air (a sphere above the earth); and so shall we ever be together (at once at the same place) with the Lord.* (18) *Wherefore comfort one another with these words.* And 1 John 3:2–3 says—*Dear friends, now we are children of God, and what we will be has not yet been made known. But we know that when Christ appears, we shall be like him, for we shall see him as he is.* (3) *All who have this hope in him purify themselves, just as he is pure (to sanctify oneself by the word of God just as that one, Jesus Christ is perfectly pure).*

So not only will the righteous in Christ be changed from mortality into immortality, and from corruptibility to incorruptibility, but also our sphere will be changed. Colossians 1:13 says—*Who (God) has rescued us from the domain (authority) of the darkness and transferred us into the kingdom of his son (a sphere above all heavens, the sovereignty of God's beloved son who is the head over all things to his assembly which is his body).* Therefore, it will be a complete change in appearance and place, from the darkness to the light, and from death to life everlasting, from the kingdom of Satan to the kingdom of God and His beloved son forever and forever, amen.

This is our hope as children (sons and daughters) of God begotten through Christ that if God did it for Enoch and the prolific prophet Elijah, and the resurrection of the Lord Jesus Christ, we who are righteous in Christ have that assurance as well. That, in whichever way, whether by translation or by resurrection, each one in their order as appointed by God, will be with our Lord Jesus Christ for eternity, to the praise and glory of our God and the father of our Lord Jesus Christ. Yes, the Lord Jesus Christ will gather His elect, at the same time and at the same place, to Himself. John 14:3 says—***And if I go and prepare a place for you, I will come again, and receive you unto myself; that where I am, there you may be also.*** Enoch fathered Methuselah, meaning "when he is dead, it shall be sent." Methuselah is the longest to have lived, at 969 years. Methuselah fathered Lamech, meaning "powerful." Lamech fathered Noah, meaning "rest or comfort." Noah fathered Shem, Ham, and Japheth. From these three sons of Noah was Yahweh to continue the Adamic race, and would come, through the seed of the woman (Eve), Jesus Christ.

CHAPTER 15:
THE SONS OF GOD

Genesis 6:1–2—(1) ***And it came to pass when men (the man Adam) began to multiply on the face of the earth (ground), and daughters were born unto them (Adam and Eve), (2) That the sons of God saw the daughters of men that they were fair; and they took them wives of all which they chose.*** Genesis 6 verses 1 and 2 take us back to Adam and Eve after the birth of Seth, when sons and daughters were born to Adam. Genesis 5:3–4 says—(3) ***And when Adam had lived one hundred and thirty years, he had a son in his own likeness, in his own image; and he named him Seth. (4) After Seth was born, Adam lived 800 years and had other sons and daughters.*** Now it happened that when Adam (who is referred to here because "men" in the original Hebrew text is singular) started to increase on the face of the earth; daughters were born of Adam and Eve. Now, it's these daughters of Adam and Eve who were a target of the sons of God. But to find out why these daughters of Adam and Eve were targets, we first have to find out who these sons of God were.

Well, the sons of God here were angels divinely created by God to carry out His will, and they were spirits in nature. Any created being that is divinely created can be called a son of God. John 3:6 says—*What is born of the flesh is flesh, and what is born of the spirit is spirit.* God is spirit. It is only by the divine act of creation that any created being can be called a son of God. The Lord Jesus Christ is called the Son of God because only He came into being by the divine will of God. And we are called sons of God through the divine regeneration of the spirit in Christ Jesus by which we become a new nature in Christ, by the divine will of God the Creator of all things in heaven and on earth. Adam is called the son of God in the book of Luke 3:38, which says—*The son of Enos, which was the son of Seth, which was the son of Adam, which was the son of God.* This is because Adam was a divine creation of God, and we are divinely regenerated by the spirit of God in a new nature. 1 Corinthians 5:17–18 says—(17) *Therefore, if anyone is in Christ, he is a new creation, old things have passed away; behold, new things have come.* (18) *And all things are of God, who has reconciled us to himself through Christ, and who has given us the ministry of reconciliation.* And Romans 8:14 says—*For those who are led by the Spirit of God are the sons of God.* This is why angels are called the sons of God, because they were divinely created by God to carry out His divine will. And that's why we are called the sons of God, to carry out His divine will on the earth through Christ Jesus. Wherever this expression, "the sons of God," is used in the Old Testament, it refers to the angels. But to equally divide the word of God, although these angels were created by God, they went against God and followed Lucifer the devil, who himself is an angel created by God. These are the third of the angels that followed the devil after he was cast down from the presence of God.

So with that in mind, these angels were not sent by God but were sent by the devil to corrupt the lineage of the seed of the woman who was to come and bruise the head of the serpent, the devil. The devil knew that if he could corrupt the lineage, God would not allow the seed Jesus Christ to come through that which is corrupt and that he, the devil, would prevent the Lord Jesus Christ from crushing his head. The seed of the woman in Genesis 3:15 is Jesus Christ, who is also called the Son of God. *And I will put enmity between you and the woman, and between your offspring and hers; he will crush your head, and you will strike his heel.* John 1:49 says—*Nathanael answered him, Rabbi, you are the son of God; You are the King of Israel!* Nathanael, by faith, divinely inspired by God, called the Lord Jesus Christ the Son of God, and in him all the fullness of the deity dwells bodily. Colossians 2:9 says—*For in Christ all the fullness of the Deity dwells in bodily form.* Colossians 1:15–20—(15) *The Son is the image of the invisible God, the firstborn over all creation.* (16) *For in him all things were created: things in heaven and on the earth, visible and invisible, whether thrones of dominions or rulers or authorities—all things were created through him and for him.* (17) *And he is before all things, and in him all things hold together.* (18) *And he is the head of the body, the church. He is the beginning, the firstborn from the dead, that in everything he might be preeminent.* (19) *For in him all the fullness of God was pleased to dwell,* (20) *and through him to reconcile to himself all things, whether on earth or in heaven, making peace by the blood of his cross.*

So I have given you a threefold meaning of the expression of the sons of God in the Bible—the first being the angels, the second being Jesus Christ, and the third being those in Christ who are led by the spirit . But these angels, implied as sons of God, should be distinguished from the angels who serve and minister onto God. And He says, concerning the angels, the one who makes His angels' spirits and His servants a flame of fire. Psalms 103:21–22 says—(21) *Bless the Lord (Yahweh), all you his hosts (angels), you ministers of his who do his will.* (22) *Bless the Lord, all his works, in all places of his dominion.* And Hebrews 1:14 says—*Are they not all spirits engaged in special service, sent on assignment for the sake of those who are going to inherit salvation?* These sons of God in Genesis 6:2 are called fallen angels and are now kept in bonds under the earth. Jude 6 refers to this angel, saying—*And the angels who did not keep to their own domain but deserted their proper dwelling place, he has kept in eternal bonds under the deep gloom for the judgement of the great day.* Also referred to in 2 Peter 2:4, saying—*For God did not spare even the angels who sinned. He threw them into hell, in gloomy pits of darkness, where they are being held until the day of judgement.* These fallen angels are servants of the devil sent to counter, or contradict and stop, the will of God on the earth. The devil knew the plans of God concerning the earth and his creation because he himself was an angel of the highest order concerning the administration on the earth, but though he knew the plans of God, he did not know the mind of God. 1 Corinthians 2:7–8 says—(7) *But we speak the hidden wisdom of God in a mystery, which God predestined before the ages for our glory,* (8) *which none of the rulers of this age knew; for had they known, they would not have crucified the Lord of glory.*

So now we have a clear picture and understanding of who these sons of God were, and the reason the devil sent them was to corrupt the lineage of the seed, who is Jesus Christ, by having intercourse with the daughters of Adam. Remember what God said to the serpent, the devil who is Satan, in Genesis 3:15—*And I (God) will put enmity (hostility) between you (Satan) and between the woman (Eve) and between your offspring (Eve's progeny) he (Jesus Christ) will strike on your (Satan's head) and you (Satan) will strike him (Jesus Christ) on his heel.* One part of this prophecy has been fulfilled, and that was of Satan striking Jesus Christ on his heel, and one is still in the future, and that is of Jesus Christ striking Satan, the devil, on his head. Jesus Christ was struck on His heel at Calvary by crucifixion. It was temporal, for He overcame death by resurrection and now lives for eternity. But when Jesus Christ the Lord strikes the devil on his head, he will not resurrect from it. That will be it for the devil for eternity.

Genesis 6:3—*And the Lord (Yahweh) said, my spirit shall not always strive with man (the man Adam), for that he also is flesh; yet his days shall be an hundred and twenty years.* Again the focus and emphasis are on Adam, and the word "man" has the article and is singular in the Hebrew text, which points to the man Adam. So Yahweh said to Adam, for that he (emphatic Adam) is also flesh, implying that Adam is also flesh just like the other men in their erring from imprudence; that lack of discernment, being easily deceived and erring willfully through being lost, and thereby going astray from the prescribed divine order of things. This is what is called the lust of the flesh—desire of the things of this world age and not of the divine will of God. The man Adam was a specific divine creation of God, different from the rest of humanity. Yahweh knew the man Adam was also able to be easily deceived for the lack of discernment, and thereby erring and going astray from the divine order of things divinely prescribed by God. Yahweh wouldn't let His spirit ("*ruach*"—the imparted breath of life) remain in the man Adam because the man Adam, as well as the rest of humankind, had corrupted their way. Therefore, what Yahweh God had declared in Genesis 2:17 that Adam shall surely die was now made clear, though he had lived 810 years. Yet his years at this time of his life were 120.

Genesis 6:4—***There were giants (Nephilim) in the earth in those days; and also after that, when the sons of God came unto the daughters of men, and they (the daughters) bare children to them, the same became mighty men which were of old, men of renown.*** These giants are called "Nephilim" in Hebrew, meaning "fallen one." They were the children born from the fallen angels (the sons of God) referred to in Jude 6 and 2 Peter 2:4, in those days of Noah, and also after that, the flood of Noah. After God destroyed these Nephilim by the flood of Noah, there was another irruption of the fallen angels (the sons of God) after the flood of Noah and they came and had intercourse with the daughters of the descendants of Adam and, again, the reason being to corrupt the bloodline of the seed of the woman Eve, through whom the seed Jesus Christ would come.

The devil had sent his evil angels to prevent the coming of this particular seed. These same Nephilim became mighty and were great in size, and also great in wickedness. They were super beings, abnormal beings. A good example of the giants is Goliath, who was killed by David. They were also called the Canaanites and Perizzites who settled in the Promised Land before Abraham. The devil knew beforehand that Yahweh would call Abram (who would later be called Abraham by God) from the land of Ur of the Chaldees (Babylonians) to the Promised Land, which Yahweh would give to Abraham and his descendants. So the devil made sure that this land was occupied in advance by his own (children) to prevent Abraham from the fulfillment of this land (the Promised Land) Yahweh promised to Abraham and his descendants. The land was called Canaan by the name of these giants who were also called men of renown, which means in Hebrew, "the men of names." They were renowned by their wickedness and size.

Genesis 6:5—*And God saw that the wickedness of man (humanity) was great (multiplied) in the earth and that every imagination of the thoughts of his heart was only evil continually.* God Yahweh perceived that the lewdness and moral depravity of humanity multiplied forcefully upon the earth and that inclination of the thoughts, motives, and intent was only inclined continually to breaking up all that was good and desirable to please Yahweh and, by so doing, became reprobates and good for nothing.

Genesis 6:6—*The Lord (Yahweh) regretted that he had made human beings on the earth, and his heart was deeply troubled.* Yahweh regretted that he had made humankind on the earth to the point that he was saddened within himself. The only thing left for Yahweh was to wipe out humankind and every created thing on the earth.

Genesis 6:7–8—*And the Lord said, I will destroy (wipe out) man whom I have created from the face of the earth (ground); both man (humankind), and beast (animals), and the creeping thing (reptiles), and the fowls of the air (birds); for it repenteth (grieves) me that I have made them. (8) But Noah found grace (favor) in the eyes of the Lord.* Only Noah was found righteous, and only his family was 100% purebred from Adam. Hebrews 11:7 says—*By faith Noah, having been warned about things not yet seen, out of reverence, constructed an ark for the deliverance of his family. By his faith he condemned the world and became heir of the righteousness that is in keeping with faith.* And 2 Peter 2:5 says—*And God did not spare the ancient world--except for Noah and the seven others in his family. Noah warned the world of*

God's righteous judgement. So, God protected Noah when he destroyed the world of ungodly people with a vast flood. So not only was Noah righteous, but Yahweh preserved him and his family because only he and his family were a pure breed from the man Adam. Through Noah's chosen family was now the seed from the woman (Eve), that Jesus Christ would come.

Genesis 6:9–10—(9) *These are the generations of Noah. Noah was a righteous man, blameless in his generation. Noah walked (to and fro habitually) with God.* (10) *And Noah had three sons; Shem, Ham, and Japheth.* This is the family history or record of Noah. He was a righteous man in the sight of God and he was without defect as to breed or pedigree. He was a pure breed from Adam, and so was his family because all flesh was corrupted in his generation. The word "perfect" in the Hebrew text here means "without blemish or defect" and pertains to bodily and physical perfection but not moral perfection. And it's the same word used for sacrificial animals. So only Noah and his family had preserved their breed and kept it pure in spite of the prevailing corruption brought about by the fallen angels. Noah had fathered three sons: Shem, Ham, and Japheth. "Walked with God" means living life habitually in the ways of God. That's why it's said that Noah was a righteous man. The sons of Noah are not named in order of their age. "Japheth," meaning "enlargement," was the oldest; then "Ham," meaning "heat" or "black" was the middle child; and the youngest was "Shem," meaning "fame (renown)." Shem's name is put first because through him God would continue His will.

Genesis 6:11–18—(11) *The earth also was corrupt before God, and the earth was filled with violence.* The earth, as created by God, was being destroyed by the maliciousness that was being done in the generation that caused the disruption of the divinely established order of things appointed by God. (12) *And God looked upon the earth, and, behold, it was corrupt; for all flesh had corrupted his way upon the earth.* And God saw that the earth was in ruin because all flesh had ruined its way on the earth, and was going astray perpetually, but only Noah's family was accepted. (13)

And God said unto Noah, The end of all flesh is come before me; for the earth is filled with violence through them; and, behold, I will destroy them with the earth. God (Elohim) the Creator said to Noah, "The end of all humankind has come to my attention due to the fullness of the depravity that has cursed the earth to be in ruin through them. Look, I will wipe them out along with the earth." (14) *Make thee an ark of gopher wood; rooms shalt thou make in the ark, and shalt pitch it within and without pitch.* God said to Noah, "Make for yourself a floating building out of gopher wood with nests, and coat it inside and out with resin, which is a mixture of bitumen or asphalt used as cement, and leaves from a henna plant for dyeing." (15) *And this is the fashion thou shalt make it of: The length of the ark shall be three hundred cubits, the breadth of it fifty cubits, and the height of it thirty cubits.* A cubit is approximately twenty-five inches. So in today's terms that would say—*This is how you are to make it: The ark will be 450 feet long, 75 feet wide and 45 feet high.* (16) *A window shalt thou make to the ark, and in a cubit shalt thou finish it above; and the door of the ark shalt thou set in the side thereof; with lower, second, and third stories shalt thou make it.* This was to be a window, literally a place for light to come through, on top of the floating building of three stories high. (17) *And, behold, I, even I, do bring a flood of waters upon the earth, to destroy all flesh, wherein is the breath of life, from under heaven; and every thing that is in the earth shall die.* A flood is a deluge of water that flows and overwhelms or inundates the ground. So by this deluge of water, God would wipe out all kinds of beings that had the breath of life in them.

(18) *But with thee I will establish my covenant; and thou shalt come into the ark, thou, and thy sons, and thy wife, and thy sons' wives with thee.* This is the first occurrence of the word "covenant," which means "confederate." Therefore, a league or alliance, but God's alliance with Noah was not from generation to generation. It was by God that he would never again wipe out all living beings that had breath of life in them, by a flood or deluge of flowing water on the earth. The sign of the covenant was a bow in the clouds, which we call a rainbow. Genesis 9:12–13 says—(12)

And God (Elohim) said, this is the token (sign) of the covenant which I have made between me and you, and every living creature (being) that is with you for all future (perpetual) generations: (13) *I have set (grant) my bow in the cloud, and it shall be a token (sign) of the covenant between me and the earth.* A bow is figuratively a bending; hence, as in bows and arrows. God did not call it a rainbow but just a bow, a bending of colors in the clouds, but as everything God meant for good, the devil always finds a way to pervert it. The world has perverted this divine sign of God's covenant with the earth to be a symbol to celebrate their unnatural, deviant, perverted acts.

Genesis 6:19—*And of every living thing of all flesh, two of every sort shalt thou bring into the ark, to keep them alive with thee; they shall be male and female.* Now, the question that can be asked is: if God wiped out all living things of all flesh, including humankind, with the flood of Noah's time, and only preserved Noah, his wife, and their three sons, and the wives of their three sons, where, then, did all the other races come from other than the Adamic race preserved through Noah's family? Well, the answer is given in the preceding verse. God said of every living thing of all flesh, including humankind of all races, two of every sort of living thing of all flesh, male and female, humankind included, was to be brought in the ark for preservation and continuation of life after the flood. There were races other than the Adamic race living before the flood that God created in Genesis 1:26. God said, "Let us make man." This word "man" in the Hebrew text means "Adam," which means "mankind" and is different than the man in Genesis 1:27, which is singular and means this same man Adam in the Hebrew text. There have been so many questions and instances of misinformation, especially when it comes to the black race. Some have said that the black race came from one of the sons of Noah—Ham, because his name means "black" in Hebrew. And some have also speculated that the black race is descended from Canaan, one of the sons of Ham who Noah cursed and had said because of that curse, the black race was cursed. Well, we know everything that God created and made was very good, beautiful, and excellent, according to Genesis 1:31.

As I have pointed out, whatever God meant for good, the devil uses it for evil. He uses racism to separate races and then turns them against each other. It's easy for him to conquer when there is division and confusion, and we know as Christians that there is neither Jew nor Greek in Christ Jesus. Christianity knows no color and no boundary.

One thing we have to know is that God does not know us by the color of our skin but by our soul and spirit. Though he predestined where we were born and who our parents must be according to his will, the color of our skin means nothing to God. God is impartial, and so should we be as Christians, and we should be able to call out injustice and partiality in the world, but especially in the church of God. Nor should the church of God be used for political and social endeavors. We, as the body of Christ, must stand on the word of God and call out what is not of God.

One thing I have noticed is that the Evangelical churches are quick to condemn abortion, which we should all do as Christians, but when it comes to racism and injustice; they tend to look the other way. We do well to speak out against abortion if by any chance we serve even one child by doing so. We should do even more when that child is born, to protect that child against racism and injustice. And all the elements of this perverted generation and at the same time, the Catholic Church do well helping the needy and the poor, and the immigrants, but when it comes to homosexuality and pedophiles in the church, they look the other way. All I'm saying is, if we are the body of Christ who knew no sin, we should condemn all that is against the word of God. We should not pick and choose what is more popular to keep a congregation. Abortion is sin, racism is sin, injustice is sin, homosexuality is sin, pedophilia is sin.

We should call sin by its name if we are truly the church of God and the body of Christ. For we know that not all churches are of God, because there are also churches of Satan in the world, according to Revelation 2:9 pertaining to the church of God—***I know thy works, and tribulation, and poverty, (but thou art rich) and I know the blasphemy of them which say they are Jews, and are not, but are the synagogue of Satan.*** Genesis 6:20–

22—(20) ***Of fowls after their kind, and of cattle after their kind, of every creeping thing of the earth (ground) after his kind, two of every sort shall come unto thee, to keep them alive.*** (21) ***And take thou unto thee of all food that is eaten, and thou shalt gather it to thee; and it shall be for food for thee, and for them.*** (22) ***Thus did Noah; according to all that God commanded him, so did he.*** Noah, by faith, believed God and did all God commanded him to do. We believe by faith knowing that whatever God says, it shall be done. And so Noah and his wife and their sons and the sons' wives, and two of each sort of animals both male and female, humankind included, entered the floating building on the second month of the year, on the seventeenth day of the month. This is symbolic of the Passover when Yahweh God delivered the Israelite from the Pharaoh in Egypt. The blood of the lamb was their covering, and during the flood, the floating building was Noah and his family's covering. Noah was six hundred years old when he and his family entered the floating building, when God let the fountains of the abyss break loose and the floodgates of heaven were opened. And it rained on the earth forty days and forty nights—forty being the number of probation, as in the forty years of the Israelites wandering in Exodus, and the forty days of the Lord Jesus in the wilderness being tested by the devil. The flood was on the earth one hundred and fifty days, that's five months—five being the number of grace. All the animals that had a breath of life ceased to breathe, including all mankind, and every standing thing was destroyed. God (Elohim the Creator) remembered Noah, not that He forgot, but the word "remembered" is used here in respect of God's promise to His covenant with Noah and all living things that He will never again destroy the earth with a flood of water.

So He closed the fountains of the abyss and restrained the rain from the heavens, and He caused a wind to blow over the earth; the water started to recede from the earth gradually. After one hundred fifty days (five months), the floating building rested at Mount Ararat on the Sabbath day, on the seventeenth day of the seventh month, exactly seven months from the beginning of the flood; the number seven being the number of spiritual completeness or perfection. This is why numbers are very important to understand and know. In the second month is Passover and in the seventh month is the feast of tabernacle or trumps—two important holy days in the Hebrew calendar. And I believe that the Lord Jesus Christ was born in the seventh month and his return will be either during Passover or during the seventh month on a day of atonement (Yom Kippur) in the Hebrew calendar, which is the second month in the Gregorian calendar and used by most of the world, which is between March and April, and the seventh is between September and October.

The Gregorian calendar was instituted by the Roman Catholic Church and was named after Pope Gregory XIII in October 1582. This calendar is perverted in that it puts Sunday as the day of worship to worship their "Sun god," instead of Saturday, according to God's calendar. Hence, the name Sunday is named after their Sun god. I've got so much to say about the Catholic Church, but that's for another time. So in all, it took one full solar calendar year from Genesis 7:11 to Genesis 8:14 for the water to dry on the earth. All the dates given pertaining to the period of the flood are Sabbaths except one in Genesis 8:5, "Sabbath" being the seventh day of the week; the number seven, again, being the number of spiritual perfection or completeness. So after a year from the beginning of the flood to the earth being dry, the Lord told Noah to come out of the floating building; he and his wife, and three sons and their wives, and all of every living thing of flesh so that they could replenish the earth. Noah built an altar, a place of worship, and gave burnt offerings to God. And God established his covenant with Noah and his seed after him, and with every living creature (soul) that is humankind and that is with you: the birds, the domesticated animals and every wild animal of the earth that came out of the floating building. After the flood, Noah lived three hundred fifty years. God's covenant continued with his three sons, Shem, Ham, and Japheth, and from these three the whole Adamic race scattered over the whole earth. But before they scattered, all people of the whole world (earth) spoke one language.

Now, let's look at the family history of each of these three sons of Noah. Genesis 10:1—***These are the generations of the sons of Noah:***

Shem, Ham, and Japheth, and unto them were sons born after the flood. Japheth was the oldest. Genesis 10:21—***Unto Shem also, the father of all the children of Eber, the brother of Japheth the elder, even to him were children born. Shem was the ancestor of all the descendants of Eber.*** The seven sons of Japheth were Gomer, Magog, Madai, Javan, Tubal, Meshech, and Tiras. And Ham was the second—Genesis 9:24—***When Noah awoke from his wine stupor, he learned what Ham, his younger (younger than Japheth) son, had done to him.*** And Shem was the youngest—Genesis 11:10—***These are the generations of Shem: Shem was an hundred years old, and begat Arphaxad two years after the flood.*** So we see the sons born to them were born after the flood but before the scattering of Genesis 11:8—***So the Lord scattered them abroad from thense upon the face of all the earth; and they left off to build the city.*** Genesis 11:2—***And it came to pass, as they journeyed from the east, that they found a plain in the land of Shinar; and they dwelt there.*** The sons of Japheth were scattered north of the Mediterranean Sea, after the Tower of Babel, and made up what is today Europe and Middle Asia, each according to his own language by their own families in their nations.

Genesis 10:6—***And the son of Ham; Cush, and Mizraim, and Phut, and Canaan.*** The sons of Ham were scattered south of the Mediterranean Sea after the Tower of Babel, and make up what is today North Africa. Cush today is Ethiopia, and Mizraim today is Egypt, Phut today is Libyia, and Canaan today is Syria. From the descendants of Ham came Babylon. This was the beginning of all false religious and worship of idols after the flood.

Genesis 10:8–10—(8) ***And Cush begat Nimrod; he began to be a mighty one (warrior) in the earth.*** (9) ***He was a mighty hunter before the Lord: wherefore it is said, Even as Nimrod the mighty hunter before the Lord.*** (10) ***And the beginning of his kingdom was Babel, and Erech, and Accad, and Calneh, in the land of Shinar.*** The name Nimrod means to rebel. He became a mighty warrior, not in a good sense but in defiance to the Lord. His kingdom included Babel, which is Babylon and Nineveh which was the capital of Assyria. Babel is the Gate of God and means "confusion," and these are also the descendants of today's Palestinians.

Genesis 10:21—*Unto Shem also, the father of all the children of Eber (Hebrews), the brother of Japheth the elder, even to him were children born.* Shem was the youngest and, through him, the lineage of the seed of the woman, Jesus Christ would come, and the rest of the book of Genesis from here is through Shem and his descendants. Genesis 10:22–24—(22) *The children of Shem; Elam, and Asshur, and Arphaxad, and Lud, and Aram. (23) And the children of Aram; Uz, and Hul, and Gether, and Mash. (24) And Arphaxad begat Salah; and Salah begat Eber.* Eber is where the name "Hebrew" is derived from, so Shem is the father of the Hebrews, and the first one to be called the Hebrew was Abram in Genesis 14:13. *And there came one that had escaped, and told Abram the Hebrew; for he dwelt in the plain of Mamre the Amorite, brother of Eshcol, and brother of Aner; and these were confederate with Abram.*

Genesis 10:25—*And unto Eber were born two sons; the name of one was Peleg, for in his days was the earth divided, and his brother's name was Joktan.* "*Peleg*" means to cleave, hence division. As so, we see the continuation of the lineage of the seed of the woman (Eve) that was to come through Shem, then Eber, and then Peleg, and from Peleg to Nahor, Nahor to Terah, and Terah to Abram, then Isaac and Jacob; all the way to the seed from the woman Eve who would bring forth Jesus the Christ; hence, the genealogy of Jesus Christ in Matthew 1:1–16—(1) *The book of the generation of Jesus Christ, the son of David, the son of Abraham. (2) Abraham begat Isaac, and Isaac begat Jacob, and Jacob begat Judas and his brethren; (3) And Judas begat Phares begat Esrom, and Esrom begat Aram; (4) And Aram begat Aminadab, and Aminadab begat Naasson, and Naasson begat Salmon; (5) And Salmon begat Booz of Rachab, and Booz begat Obed of Ruth, and Obed begat Jesse; (6) And Jesse begat David the king, and David the king begat Solomon of her that had been the wife of Urias; (7) And Solomon begat Roboam, and Roboam begat Abia, and Abia begat Asa; (8) And Asa begat Josaphat, and Josaphat begat Joram, and Joram begat Ozias; (9) And Ozias begat Joatham, and Joatham begat Achaz, and Achaz begat Ezekias; (10) And Ezekias begat Manasses, and Manasses begat Amon, and Amon begat Josias; (11) And Josias begat Jechonias and his brethren, about the time they were carried away to Babylon; (12) And after they were brought to Babylon, Jechonias begat Salathiel, and Salathiel begat Zorobabel; (13) And Zorobabel begat Abiud, and Abiud begat Eliakim, and Eliakim begat Azor; (14) And Azor begat Sadoc, and Sadoc begat Achim, and Achim begat Eliud; (15) And Eliud begat Eleazar, and Eleazar begat Matthan, and Matthan begat Jacob; (16) And Jacob begat Joseph the husband of Mary, of whom was born Jesus, who is called Christ.*

CHAPTER 16:
THE WORLD AGE THAT IS TO COME

2 Peter 3:7—***But the heavens and the earth which are now, by the same word are kept in store, reserved unto fire against the day of judgement and perdition of ungodly men.*** So just as the heavens and the earth that then were in 2 Peter 3:6 were left desolated by being submerged with water, the heavens that are now are treasured up to be destroyed by fire on the day of judgment and destruction of ungodly people. Isaiah 65:17 says—***For behold, I create new heavens and a new earth; and the former shall not be remembered, nor come into mind.*** And Isaiah 66:22 says—***For just as the new heavens and the new earth, which I will make shall stand before me, declares the Lord Yahweh, so shall your descendants and your name stand.*** God has already declared this for a fact that the heavens and the earth that are now will be shaken, and things that are corrupt will be burnt up by fire and will be made fresh (renewed). 2 Peter 3:13 says—***According to his promise, we are waiting for new heavens and a new earth in which righteousness resides.*** And Revelation 21:1

says—*And I saw a new heaven and a new earth; the first heaven and the first earth were passed away, and there was no more sea.* The word "new" means "fresh," as in quality or form in the Greek text.

So the heavens and the earth of Genesis 1:1, which were of old, are still the same heavens and earth that are now and that will be made new by being refreshed, and this refreshed heaven and earth are everlasting. This will take place after the one-thousand-year rule of the Lord here on the earth after the devil and the ungodly people will be thrown in the lake of fire, which is the last death, and after that there will be no death, for all who will be found righteous will have everlasting life (bodies). But there is a period of a thousand years from the coming of the Lord Jesus Christ to set up his kingdom on the earth and to rule. The new heavens and earth God will establish after all that offends has been thrown into the lake of fire. This is when the New Jerusalem will come down from God out of heaven; this is the Tabernacle of God, the city above. Galatians 4:26—*But Jerusalem which is above is free, which is the mother of us all.* And which has the foundation of that which Abraham saw and was expecting by faith. Hebrews 11:10 says—*For he looked for a city which hath foundations, whose builder and maker is God.* And Hebrews 12:22 says—*But you have come to Mount Zion, to the city of the living God, the heavenly Jerusalem. You have come to thousands upon thousands of angels in festal gathering.* This will be the dwelling place of God on the earth. Revelation 21:3–4 says—(3) *And I heard a loud voice from the throne saying, Behold, the dwelling (Tabernacle) place of God is with man. He will dwell with them, and they will be his people, and God himself will be with them as their God.* (4) *He will wipe away every tear from their eyes, and death shall be no more, neither shall there be mourning, nor crying, nor pain anymore, for the former things have passed away.* God will make all things new. This is emphatically true, because the word of God is true, and God is not an actual man who would lie. But this new, refreshed heaven and earth are only for the righteous of old and those who die in Christ, and those who will overcome the devil and his deception in the tribulation period, and those who will accept the

King of kings and the Lord of lords as their King and Lord, and only in the thousand years of his rule on the earth. This comes with a warning: Revelation 22:11 states—***The one who does evil, let him do evil still, and the one defiled, let him be defiled still, and the righteous, let him practice righteousness still, and the holy, let him be holy still.*** The question I may ask you is, who are you of the people mentioned in this verse? If you have accepted Christ but you are living a life of sin, you need to repent and turn away from the evil of this world age so that you are not found defiled by the Lord at his coming. And those who are righteous, and the holy ones, still remain righteous and holy by faith so that you are found blameless at His coming. Revelation 21:8 says—***But as for the cowards and unbelievers, and detestable persons, and murderers, and sexually immoral people, and sorcerers, and idolaters, and all liars, their share is in the lake that burns with fire and sulphur, which is the second death.*** The second death is the death of the soul. The first death is the death of the flesh body. Revelation 22:15 says—***Outside are the dogs (false worshipers) and the sorcerers, and the sexually immoral, and murderers and idolaters, and everyone who loves and practices falsehood.***

Those of this world shall never be part of the new heavens and earth, but the principal things are living righteously and holy, which is what pleases God, and it is believers who are righteous and holy in Christ at his coming that will be snatched and transformed into a new spiritual body, and will be with the Lord forever and ever, and will not see the second death. Yet those, although they know God and accepted the Lord Jesus Christ but, who lived the life of this world are just like the ungodly of the world and will be thrown into the lake of fire at the end of His thousand-year reign on the earth as King of kings and Lord of lords, which is the Great White Throne Judgment, the judgment before God refreshes the heavens and earth, which are now, and makes them new and everlasting. Romans 1:21—***Although they knew God, they did not glorify him as God, nor were thankful, but became futile in their thoughts, and their foolish hearts were darkened.*** And Romans 1:26–32—says (26) ***Because of this, God gave them over to degrading passions, for their females exchanged*** *natural relations for those contrary to nature, (27) and likewise, also, the male, abandoning the natural relations with the female, were inflamed in their desires towards one another; male with males, committing the shameless deed, and receiving in themselves the penalty that was necessary for their error. (28) Furthermore, just as they did not think it worthwhile to retain the knowledge of God, so God gave them over to a depraved mind, so that they do what ought not to be done. (29) They have become filled with every kind (all acts of sin) of wickedness, evil, greed and depravity. They are full of envy, murder (slaughter), strife, deceit and malice. They are gossips, (30) slanderers, God-haters, insolent boldly rude or disrespectful), arrogant (proud) and boastful; they invent ways of doing evil (schemers of evil); they disobey their parents; (31) they have no understanding (unintelligent), no fidelity, no love, no mercy (hardhearted even towards kindred). (32) Although they know God's righteous decree that those who do such things deserve death, they not only continue to do these very things but also approve of those who practice them.*

A warning to those who know the requirements of God, through the word of God, but practice these wicked and evil acts, and also to those not practicing these wicked and evil acts but who approve or accept these habitual or perpetual practices, these things are just the same as for those who do practice them (these same acts). This is a warning for pastors who allow people in their church knowing that they are homosexuals, practice sexual immorality, and all other forms of evil and wicked practices in the church, for they will receive the same judgment as those practicing these evil acts, but also we as born-again Christians should not approve or accept people in our lives who perpetually live a life of sin, especially those who claim to know God, but we should not close our hearts to them, because just maybe we can bring them to repentance by preaching to them the requirements of God through His word so that they may repent and turn and give themselves to Christ, who is our hope for the new heaven and earth. We should stand firm on the word of God by being an example of a wall of righteousness living life in Christ. Not only an example, but we should also be able to share the truth with those who are living the life of this world age that those who live such a life will not have a part in the new heaven and earth. 1 Corinthians 6:9–10 says—(9) *Do you not know that the wicked will not inherit the kingdom of God? Do not be deceived; neither the sexually immoral, nor idolaters, nor adulterers, nor men who have sex with men,* (10) *nor thieves, nor the greedy, nor drunkards, nor slanderers, nor swindlers will inherit the kingdom of God.* And Proverbs 24:1 says—*Do not envy men (people) of evil, and do not desire to be with them.* 1 Corinthians 15:33 states—*Do not be deceived; bad company corrupts good character (morals).* And Galatians 6:7 says—*Do not be deceived; God is not being mocked, for whatever one (a person) sows, that will he also reap.* 1 John 2:15–17 says—(15) *Do not love the world or anything in the world. If anyone loves the world, love for the Father is not in them.* (16) *For everything in the world—the lust of the flesh, the lust of the eyes, and the pride of life—comes not from the Father but from the world.* (17) *The world and its desires pass away, but whoever does the will of God lives forever.* And Jude 21–23 says—(21) *Keep yourselves in the love of God looking forward to the mercy of our Lord Jesus Christ to eternal life,* (22) *and have mercy on those who doubt;* (23) *save others by snatching them from the fire, to others show mercy, mixed with fear—hating even the clothing stained by corrupted flesh.*

Fathers, mothers, brothers, and sisters in the Lord Jesus Christ, this is the word of God. It is true and it is life; it has been tested and proved, for God is not a man that He would lie. It is spiritual in nature and it is everlasting, life-changing and life-giving. It has changed my life from the life of this world to the life of the kingdom of God. Six years ago, in 2015, my life was so bleak; everything I tried to do, even with good intensions, I would find myself in wrong relationships with women, after going through a divorce and being a single father of three children. But in all this and through all this, God had grace upon me. I did not know how I made it all those years being a single father without any financial help from the mother of my children. I worked two jobs with three children aged ten, seven, and two years old. I would wake up and get my two older children ready for school, and then I would get my two-year-old ready, feed him, and take him to the babysitter. Then I would go to my part-time job for four hours in the morning. After I got off work there, I would go and pick up my two-year-old son from the babysitter, go home, feed him, then drop him off at the babysitter's again. I would then go to my full-time job as a caregiver in a group home. When my two oldest kids would get out of school, I would have them dropped off at the babysitter's. And then when I got off work at 10:00 PM, I would go and pick all of them up from the babysitter's. Once we got home, I would make sure they were ready for the next day to do it all over again. And once they were in bed, I would start cooking their dinner for the next day, shower, and go to bed around midnight. That was my routine and my life, but the older they got, the easier it became. I thank the almighty God for His grace and giving me the strength to endure all those years. I know now that I would have not done it efficiently without His grace. My kids lacked nothing; it was the best time of my life, and I will forever treasure those years as difficult and challenging as they were.

After seven years of being a single father, my oldest son being seventeen years, my daughter being fourteen, and my youngest son at nine years old, their mother came to pick them up for Christmas, and while they were there, she decided that they should stay and live with her. It was a tough time for both me and especially my children because they were used to me. But as tough as it was, I had to give their mother a chance to be in their lives. My life suddenly felt so empty. I was by myself and I didn't know what to do with my life. I would visit my kids every month, which was a four-hour drive from Pittsburgh, Pennsylvania, to Baltimore, Maryland. I got in a relationship with a lady in Chicago that was a long-distance relationship, and so after some time, I moved to Chicago to live with her. It was the worst decision I made, and after three years with her, I had to move out. It was during those three years that I was trying to find myself. I felt out of place most of the time around people I just couldn't fit in with.

That's the time I started seeking God. I was prompted by the spirit to move and separate myself from anyone and anything that did not align with righteousness. He (Jesus) gave me the gift of discernment to discern people around me who didn't belong in my life. So I separated and cut off anyone who I discerned not to be in the righteousness of God in Christ. I was all alone but not lonely because the Lord was with me. He had always been with me, but I was just caught up in the filthiness of this world and with the wrong people. He gave me the appetite to know of His word and I started reading and studying the Bible, and I fell in love with it. The gospel has become my life, and the Lord Jesus Christ has become the love of my soul, and of my life. I live by every word that proceeds out of the mouth of God. I have found what I have always been longing for; my God and my Lord, Oh how I love Him. I have found fulfillment in Christ. The word of God says, in Matthew 6:33—***But seek first his kingdom and his righteousness, and all these things will be given to you as well***. Yes, I can decree that I am the righteousness of God in Christ, and I am not ashamed of His word because it is a life worthy of living, but I still worry and pray for my children. They are all grown up now, and growing up comes with choices. I hope and pray that God will give them what He has given me—His love and peace in Christ—and that I may live to be an example of Christ in me, the hope of glory.

If I may leave you with something, I leave you with this assurance and hope for the coming of the Lord, and the new heaven and earth. Revelation 21:1–7—(1) ***And I saw a new heaven and a new earth; for the first heaven and the first earth were passed away, and there was no more sea. (2) And I John saw the holy city, New Jerusalem, coming down from God out of heaven, prepared as a bride adorned for her husband. (3) And I heard a great voice out of heaven saying, Behold, the tabernacle of God is with men, and he will dwell with them, and they shall be his people, and God himself shall be with them, and be their God. (4) And God shall wipe away all tears from their eyes, and there shall be no more death, neither sorrow, nor crying, neither shall there be any more pain; for the former things are passed away. (5) And he that sat upon*** *the throne said, Behold, I make all things new. And he said unto me, Write; for these words are true and faithful. (6) And he said unto me, It is done. I am the Alpha and Omega, the beginning and the end. I will give unto him that is athirst (thirsty) of the fountain of the water of life freely. (7) He that overcometh shall inherit all things; and I will be his God, and he shall be my son.* And He will wipe away every tear from our eyes, and death will not exist any longer, and mourning, wailing, and pain no longer will exist. Revelation 22:17 says—*And the spirit and the bride (the New Jerusalem) say, Come! And let him that heareth say, Come! And let him that is athirst (thirsty) come. And whosoever will, let him take the water of life freely.* Amen, come, Lord Jesus.

www.ingramcontent.com/pod-product-compliance
Lightning Source LLC
Chambersburg PA
CBHW051223160726
47994CB00002B/731